Cognitive Computing with IBM Watson

Build smart applications using artificial intelligence as a service

Rob High
Tanmay Bakshi

BIRMINGHAM - MUMBAI

Cognitive Computing with IBM Watson

Commissioning Editor: Sunith Shetty
Acquisition Editor: Devika Battike
Content Development Editor: Nathanya Dias
Technical Editor: Utkarsha S. Kadam
Copy Editor: Safis Editing
Project Coordinator: Kirti Pisat
Proofreader: Safis Editing
Indexer: Pratik Shirodkar
Graphics: Jisha Chirayil
Production Designer: Nilesh Mohite

First published: April 2019

Production reference: 2270619

Published by Packt Publishing Ltd.
Livery Place
35 Livery Street
Birmingham
B3 2PB, UK.

ISBN 978-1-78847-829-8

www.packtpub.com

Subscribe to our online digital library for full access to over 7,000 books and videos, as well as industry leading tools to help you plan your personal development and advance your career. For more information, please visit our website.

Why subscribe?

- Spend less time learning and more time coding with practical eBooks and Videos from over 4,000 industry professionals

- Improve your learning with Skill Plans built especially for you

- Get a free eBook or video every month

- Fully searchable for easy access to vital information

- Copy and paste, print, and bookmark content

Did you know that Packt offers eBook versions of every book published, with PDF and ePub files available? You can upgrade to the eBook version at www.packt.com and as a print book customer, you are entitled to a discount on the eBook copy. Get in touch with us at customercare@packtpub.com for more details.

At www.packt.com, you can also read a collection of free technical articles, sign up for a range of free newsletters, and receive exclusive discounts and offers on Packt books and eBooks.

Contributors

About the authors

Rob High is an IBM Fellow and CTO of IBM's Edge Computing business. Previously, he was CTO for IBM Watson, responsible for setting the technical strategy and vision for IBM's leadership in AI computing. High is recognized as a global technical leader, author, and evangelist, and was named an IBM Fellow in 2008 for his pioneering work in the field of SOA and for his leadership on WebSphere.

Tanmay Bakshi is a cognitive computing and AI developer, a keynote and TED speaker, an algorithm-ist, a YouTuber, IBM Champion for Cloud, an Honorary IBM Cloud Advisor, and a Google Developer Expert for Machine Learning. He has resolved to reach out to and help at least 100,000 novices and beginners so they can learn how to code.

About the reviewer

Mayur Narkhede has good blend of experience in data science and industry. He is a researcher with a B.Tech in Computer Science and an M.Tech. in Computer Science Engineering with a specialization in artificial intelligence.

Mayur is a data scientist with experience of building automated, end-to-end solutions. He is proficient at applying technology, AI, machine learning, data mining, and design thinking for better understanding and predictions in order to improve business functions and to meet the desired requirements with a growth in profitability.

He has worked on multiple advanced solutions, such as machine learning and predictive model development for oil and gas, utilities, financial services, road traffic and transport, life science, and big data platforms for asset-intensive industries. He also played a key role in setting up the Data Science and Big Data lab for R&D work. He has built solutions in areas such as asset health monitoring, batch process performance analysis, smart metering for water utility clients, predictive model development for oil and gas customers, big data platforms for asset-intensive industries, a traffic prediction algorithm for top Indian cities, and clustered graph algorithms for life sciences.

He likes to play badminton and carrom, and sometimes he goes trekking, and loves to travel new places.

Packt is searching for authors like you

If you're interested in becoming an author for Packt, please visit `authors.packtpub.com` and apply today. We have worked with thousands of developers and tech professionals, just like you, to help them share their insight with the global tech community. You can make a general application, apply for a specific hot topic that we are recruiting an author for, or submit your own idea.

Table of Contents

Preface   1

Chapter 1: Background, Transition, and the Future of Computing   7
  Transitioning from conventional to cognitive computing   8
    Limitations of conventional computing   8
      Solving conventional computing's problems   10
  Workings of machine learning   11
    Machine learning and its uses   12
      Cons of machine learning   13
  Introduction to IBM Watson   16
    Hardware and software requirements   17
      Signing up for IBM Cloud   17
  Summary   18

Chapter 2: Can Machines Converse Like Humans?   19
  Creating a conversational agent workspace   21
    Creating an instance of Watson Assistant and a workspace   21
    The sample application   24
  Creating a set of conversational intents   25
    Recognizing entities   33
  Identifying entities through annotators   38
  Building a dialog   40
    Creating the dialog for a complex Intent using Frame Slots 43
      Context variables   46
  Programming your conversation application   52
  Emerging features   60
  Summary   61
  Further reading   61

Chapter 3: Computer Vision   63
  Can machines visually perceive the world around them?   63
    The past – classical computer vision   64
    The present – deep learning for computer vision   65
  Creating a basic image-recognition system   66
  Creating an instance of Watson Visual Recognition and a classifier 66
    Uploading data and training the classifier   68
    Testing the classifier   70
    Creating a Python application to classify with Watson   71
    Handling the case where you don't have training data   74
    Using the facial detection model   75

Summary   79

Chapter 4: This Is How Computers Speak   81
  A computer that talks   82
    Playing sound through the speaker   84
  Getting fancier with how to speak   85
    Controlling pronunciation   86
    Customizing speech synthesis   87
    Using sounds-like customization   89
    Streaming and timing   89
  A fun application of the speech service   91
    Talking to the computer   92
    Getting voice from a microphone   93
    Using the WebSockets interface to speech recognition 96
    Telephones are not good microphones   103
    More about base models   104
    Dealing with speaker hesitations   105
  Customizing the speech recognition service   106
    Customizing Watson's language model   106
    Customizing the acoustic model for Watson   108
    Leveraging batch processing   109
  Summary   110
  Further reading   111

Chapter 5: Expecting Empathy from Dumb Computers   113
  Introducing empathy   113
    Understanding the complexities of sentiment   114
  The functionality of the Tone Analyzer API   115
    How you can use the Tone Analyzer API   116
  Understanding personality through natural language   120
    Using natural language to infer personality traits 121
  Calling the Personality Insights API   123
  Summary   125

Chapter 6: Language - How Watson Deals with NL   127
  Natural language translation – the past   128
    Natural language – it's intrinsically unstructured 128
  Natural language translation – the present   131
  Translating between languages with Language Translator   138
  Training custom NMT models with Watson   139
  Categorizing text using Natural Language Classifier   140
  Summary   149
  Further reading   150

Chapter 7: Structuring Unstructured Content Through Watson   151
  Using computers that recognize what you mean   152

Introducing the NLU service 153
  Alternative sources of literature 156
  Types of analyses 157
    Categories 158
  Concepts 159
    Emotion 160
    Sentiment 161
    Entities 161
    Relations 163
    Keywords 164
    Semantic roles 164
    Parts of speech (syntax) 165
Customizing NLU 167
  Preparing to annotate 168
  Creating a type system 170
  Adding documents 174
    As an aside 175
  Preparing documents for use in Watson Knowledge Studio 176
  Loading documents into Watson Studio 177
    Performing annotations 180
    Editing the type system 187
    The importance of being thorough 189
    Coreferences 190
    Training Watson 193
    Deploying the custom model to NLU 198
Using a custom model in NLU 200
Summary 202

Chapter 8: Putting It All Together with Watson 203
Recapping Watson Services 204
Building a sample application from Watson Services 205
  The use case and application 206
  The program flow 207
    Translating voice input 209
    Determining intent 211
    Prompting the user for their input 212
    Setting the document of interest 214
    Summarizing entities and concepts 216
    Identifying an entity of interest 216
    Assessing the personality of the entity 217
    Assessing the tone of the entity 217
    Translating text 218
    Classifying text 218
Running the program 218
  Setup 219
Summary 221

Chapter 9: Future - Cognitive Computing and You 223

Other services and features of Watson   224
   Compare and Comply   224
   Discovery   225
   Watson Studio   226
   Machine learning   226
   Knowledge catalog   227
   Watson OpenScale   227
The future of Watson   228
Advances in AI   229
   Generative adversarial networks   229
   Conversational systems   230
   Deep learning   231
   Edge computing   232
   Bias and ethics in AI   232
   Robotics and embodiment   233
   Quantum computing and AI   234
The future of AI   235
Summary   237

Another Book You May Enjoy   239

Index   241

Preface

Cognitive computing is rapidly infusing every aspect of our lives. It relates to the three important fields of data science, machine learning, and **artificial intelligence** (**AI**). It allows computing systems to learn and keep on improving with the growing data in the system.

This book will introduce the readers to a whole new paradigm of computing that is totally different from the conventional computing of the Information Age. You will learn about the concepts of machine learning, deep learning, neural networks, and AI through the set of DLaaS APIs that IBM Watson provides. This book will show you how to build your own applications that will understand, plan, decide, solve problems, analyze, synthesize, and assess task as per your needs. You will be exposed to various domains of cognitive computing, such as **natural language processing** (**NLP**), media analytics, embedded deep learning, computer vision, emotion analytics, and situational awareness using different IBM Watson APIs, such as the conversation API and the Visual Recognition API. You'll also build sentiment analysis apps using the Tone Analyzer API, and explore the Personality Insights API, among others.

This way, readers will be elevated to a level where they can fully understand what machine learning is, and what goes on behind the scenes to make computers do their magic, as well as the areas where these concepts can be applied. Having achieved this, readers will then be able to embark upon their journey of learning, researching, or applying the concepts they have learned to their respective fields.

Who this book is for

This book is for beginners and novices; having some knowledge of AI and deep learning is an advantage, but not a prerequisite to benefit from this book. We explain the concepts of deep learning, **Deep Learning as a Service** (**DLaaS**), and AI through the set of tools that IBM Watson provides.

What this book covers

Chapter 1, *Background, Transition and the Future of Computing*, covers what conventional computing is, its limitations, and why we need cognitive computing. It also covers the downsides of conventional computing from different angles.

Chapter 2, *Can Machines Converse Like Humans?*, looks at conversations through machines and the concept of devices conversing with humans like humans, which goes into the chatbots you use every day.

Chapter 3, *Computer Vision*, discusses how computers can be given the ability to see something and make decisions to help us in tasks such as recognizing, categorizing, and alerting.

Chapter 4, *This Is How Computers Speak*, is about how computers convert text to speech and vice versa.

Chapter 5, *Expecting Empathy from Dumb Computers*, introduces the concept of empathy, as we understand it, and what we can expect from computers in terms of emotion and personal judgment.

Chapter 6, *Language - How Watson Deals with NL*, covers the discovery and understanding of unstructured content via cognitive metadata. This includes two subtopics—the discovery service, and natural language understanding.

Chapter 7, *Structuring Unstructured Content Through Watson*, is about four APIs that Watson provides, namely, language translator, natural language classifier, document conversion, and retrieve and rank.

Chapter 8, *Putting It All Together with Watson*, will introduce an application that demonstrates the use of many of the Watson services that we have covered in this book. This will demonstrate how these services can be brought together to achieve a simple, but interesting and useful application of those services.

Chapter 9, *Future - Cognitive Computing and You*, considers where cognitive computing is headed, and discusses some use cases in the fields of robotics and simulations, along with what you should do to move forward after completing this book. This chapter guides the reader by citing resources and providing tips about how to plan your next steps; which companies to look at for further research and jobs; and where to look if some professional help is required.

To get the most out of this book

Having some knowledge of AI and deep learning will be an advantage, but not a prerequisite, to benefit from this book.

Download the example code files

You can download the example code files for this book from your account at `www.packt.com`. If you purchased this book elsewhere, you can visit `www.packt.com/support` and register to have the files emailed directly to you.

You can download the code files by following these steps:

1. Log in or register at `www.packt.com`.
2. Select the **SUPPORT** tab.
3. Click on **Code Downloads & Errata**.
4. Enter the name of the book in the **Search** box and follow the onscreen instructions.

Once the file is downloaded, please make sure that you unzip or extract the folder using the latest version of:

- WinRAR/7-Zip for Windows
- Zipeg/iZip/UnRarX for Mac
- 7-Zip/PeaZip for Linux

The code bundle for the book is hosted on GitHub at `https://github.com/PacktPublishing/Cognitive-Computing-with-IBM-Watson`.

You can also find code files on Authors GitHub at `https://github.com/tanmayb123/cognitive-computing-with-watson`. In case there's an update to the code, it will be updated on the existing GitHub repository.

We also have other code bundles from our rich catalog of books and videos available at `https://github.com/PacktPublishing/`. Check them out!

Download the color images

We also provide a PDF file that has color images of the screenshots/diagrams used in this book. You can download it here:
`http://www.packtpub.com/sites/default/files/downloads/9781788478298_ColorImages`
`.pdf`.

Conventions used

There are a number of text conventions used throughout this book.

`CodeInText`: Indicates code words in text, database table names, folder names, filenames, file extensions, pathnames, dummy URLs, user input, and Twitter handles. Here is an example: "Mount the downloaded `WebStorm-10*.dmg` disk image file as another disk in your system."

A block of code is set as follows:

```
import json from ibm_watson.visual_recognition_v3 import
VisualRecognitionV3
```

Bold: Indicates a new term, an important word, or words that you see onscreen. For example, words in menus or dialog boxes appear in the text like this. Here is an example: "Select the **Annotate** button on your **Annotation Set.**"

Warnings or important notes appear like this.

Tips and tricks appear like this.

Get in touch

Feedback from our readers is always welcome.

General feedback: If you have questions about any aspect of this book, mention the book title in the subject of your message and email us at `customercare@packtpub.com`.

Errata: Although we have taken every care to ensure the accuracy of our content, mistakes do happen. If you have found a mistake in this book, we would be grateful if you would report this to us. Please visit www.packt.com/submit-errata, selecting your book, clicking on the Errata Submission Form link, and entering the details.

Piracy: If you come across any illegal copies of our works in any form on the Internet, we would be grateful if you would provide us with the location address or website name. Please contact us at copyright@packt.com with a link to the material.

If you are interested in becoming an author: If there is a topic that you have expertise in and you are interested in either writing or contributing to a book, please visit authors.packtpub.com.

Reviews

Please leave a review. Once you have read and used this book, why not leave a review on the site that you purchased it from? Potential readers can then see and use your unbiased opinion to make purchase decisions, we at Packt can understand what you think about our products, and our authors can see your feedback on their book. Thank you!

For more information about Packt, please visit packt.com.

Background, Transition, and the Future of Computing

1

Welcome to the world of *Cognitive Computing with IBM Watson*. We'll be starting the book by learning the answers to the following questions:

- What is AI and why do we need AI? Why can't we just use regular, traditional technologies?
- What are some examples of transitioning from regular technology to new, AI-based technology?
- Are there some disadvantages to AI technology, and can it be used in a negative fashion?
- How can I get started developing with IBM Cloud?
- What do I need in terms of hardware and software to learn through this book?

This book will also take us through some of the ways that the machine learning technology itself can be implemented for similar use cases. This book assumes you're already somewhat tech-savvy and familiar with application development and programming. We'll be going through implementations in Python, because the Watson Developer Cloud provides language-specific SDKs to access the Watson REST APIs and you mostly have a congruent coding experience, even across languages.

In this chapter, we will discuss the following topics:

- Transitioning from conventional to cognitive computing
- Limitations of conventional computing
- Solving conventional computing problems
- Workings of machine learning
- Cons of machine learning
- Introduction to IBM Watson
- Hardware and software requirements

Transitioning from conventional to cognitive computing

Currently, the world of computing is undergoing a massive shift, turning into a new plane altogether, of machine learning technology. This is the new necessity due to the massive rise in data, its complexity, and the availability of more and more computing power.

This new computing paradigm is all about finding patterns in data so complex that its problems were so far deemed to be unsolvable by computers—problems that are trivial to humans, even children, such as natural language understanding and playing games, such as chess and Go. A new kind of algorithm was needed to understand data the way a biological neural network does. This new algorithm or solution is computing, which is known as **cognitive computing**.

IBM realized the potential in machine learning even before it went mainstream, and created Watson, a set of tools that we, the developers, can use in our applications to incorporate cognitive computing without the manual implementation of that technology.

Limitations of conventional computing

Traditionally, computers have been good at one thing, and that is **mathematical logic**. They're amazing at processing mathematical operations at a rate many orders of magnitude faster than any human could ever be, or will ever be, able to. However, that in itself is a huge problem, as computers have been designed in such a way that they can't work with data if we can't express the algorithm in a set of mathematical operations that actually understands that data.

Therefore, tasks that humans find simple, such as understanding natural languages, visual, and auditory information, are practically impossible for computers to perform. Why? Well, let's take a look at the sentence *I shot an elephant in my pyjamas.*

What does that sentence mean? Well, if you were to think about it, you'd say that it means a person, *clad in his pyjamas, is taking a photograph of the elephant.* However, the sentence is ambiguous; we may assume questions such as, *Is the elephant wearing the pyjamas?*, and *Is the human hunting the elephant?* There are many different ways that we could interpret this.

However, if we take into account the fact that the person mentions that this is Tom, and that Tom is a photographer, then we know that pyjamas are usually associated with humans and that elephants and animals in general don't usually wear clothes. We can then understand the sentence the way it's meant to be understood.

The contextual resolution that went behind understanding the sentence is something that comes naturally to us humans. Natural language is something we're built to be great at understanding and it's quite literally encoded within our **Forkhead box Protein P2** (**FOXP2**) gene; it's an innate ability of ours.

 There's proof that natural language is encoded within our genes, even down to the way it's structured. Even if different languages were developed from scratch by different cultures in complete isolation from one another, they have the same, very basic, underlying structure, such as nouns, verbs, and adjectives.

But there's a problem, there's a (sometimes unclear) difference between knowledge and understanding. For example, when we ride a bike, we know how to ride a bike, but we don't necessarily understand how to ride a bike. All of the balancing, the gyroscopic movement, and tracking is a very complex algorithm that our brain runs on, without even realizing it, when we ride a bike. If we were to ask someone to write all the mathematical operations that go behind riding a bike, it would be next to impossible for them to do so, unless they're a physicist. You can find out more about this algorithm, the distinction between knowledge and understanding, how the human mind adapts, and more, with this video by **SmarterEveryDay** on YouTube: `https://www.youtube.com/watch?v=MFzDaBzBlL0`.

Similarly, we know how to understand natural language, but we don't completely understand the extremely complex algorithm that goes behind understanding it.

Since we don't understand that complex algorithm, we cannot express it mathematically and, hence, computers cannot understand natural language data, until we provide them the algorithms to do so.

Similar logic applies to visual data and auditory data, or practically any other kind of information that we, as humans, are naturally good at recognizing, but are simply unable to create algorithms for.

There are also some cases in which humans and computers can't work well with data. In a majority of the cases, this would be high-diversity tabular data with many features. A great example of this kind of data is fraud detection data, in which we have lots of features, location, price, category of purchase, and time of day, just to name a few. At the same time, however, there is a lot of diversity. Someone could buy a plane ticket once a year for a vacation, but it wouldn't be a fraudulent purchase as it was made by the owner of the card with a clear intention.

Because of the high diversity, high feature count, and the fact that it's better to be safe than sorry when it comes to this kind of fraud detection, there are numerous points at which a user could get frustrated while working with this system. A real-life example is when I was trying to order an iPhone on the launch day. As this was a very rushed ordeal, I tried to add my card to Apple Pay beforehand. Since I was trying to add my card to Apple Pay with a different verification method than the default, my card provider's algorithm thought someone was committing fraud and locked down my account. Fortunately, I still ended up getting it on launch day, using another card.

In other cases, these systems end up failing altogether, especially when we employ social engineering tricks, such as connecting with other humans on a personal level and psychologically tricking them into trusting us to get into people's accounts.

Solving conventional computing's problems

To solve computing problems, we use **machine learning** (**ML**) technology.

However, we need to remember one distinction between machine learning and artificial intelligence (AI).

By the very bare-bone definitions, AI is a term for replicating organic, or natural, intelligence (that is, the human mind) within a computer. Up until now, this has been an impossible feat due to numerous technical and physical limitations.

However, the term AI is usually confused with many other kinds of systems. Usually, the term is used for any computer system that displays the ability to do something that we thought required human intelligence.

For example, the IBM DeepBlue is the machine that played and won chess against the world champion, Garry Kasparov, in 1997. This is not artificial intelligence as it doesn't understand how to play chess; nor does it learn how to play the game. Rather, humans hardcode the rules of chess, and the algorithm plays like this:

- For this current chess board, what are all the possible moves I could make?
- For all of those boards, what are all the moves my opponent could make?
- For all of those boards, what are all the possible moves that I could make?

It'll do that over and over, until it has a tree of almost every chess board possible in this game. Then, it chooses the move that, in the end, has the least likelihood of losing, and the highest likelihood of winning for the computer.

You can call this a rule-based system, and it's a stark contrast from what AI truly is.

On the other hand, a specific type of AI, ML, gets much closer to what we think of as AI. We like to define it as creating mathematical models that transform input data into predictions. Imagine being able to represent the method through how you can determine whether a set of pixels contains a cat or dog!

In essence, instead of us humans trying our best to quantify different concepts into mathematical algorithms, the machine can do it for us. The theory is that it's a set of math that can adapt to any other mathematical function, when given enough time, energy, and data.

A perfect example of machine learning in action is IBM's DeepQA algorithm which went behind Watson when it played and won *Jeopardy!*, Watson played on the game show against the two best human competitors on the game show, namely Ken Jennings and Brad Rutter. *Jeopardy*, is a game with puns, riddles, and wordplay in each clue—clues such as *This trusted friend was the first non-dairy powdered creamer*.

If we were to analyze this from a naive perspective, we'd realize that the word friend, which is usually associated with humans, simply cannot be related to a creamer, which has the attributes **the first**, **powdered**, and **non-dairy**. However, if you were to understand the wordplay behind it, you'd realize the answer is *What is coffee mate?*, since mate means trusted friend, and coffee mate was the first non-dairy powdered creamer.

Therefore, machine learning is essentially a set of algorithms which, when combined with even more systems, such as rule-based systems one could, theoretically, help us simulate the human mind within a computer. Whether or not we'll get there is another discussion altogether, considering the physical limitations around the hardware and architecture of the computers themselves. However, we believe that not only will we not reach this stage, but it's something we wouldn't want to do in the first place.

Workings of machine learning

ML is still an umbrella term—there are many different ways in which we can implement it, namely, K-means clustering, logistic regression, linear regression, support vector machines, and many more. In this book, we'll be mainly focusing on one type of machine learning, that is, **artificial neural networks (ANNs)**.

ANN, or neural networks for short, are a set of techniques, some of which can be referred to as deep learning. It is a type of machine learning algorithm that is, at a very high-level, inspired by the structure of our biological nervous systems. By high-level, we mean that the algorithms are nowhere near to being the same. As a matter of fact, we barely understand how our nervous system learns in the first place. But even the part that was inspired by our nervous system, its structure, is still primitive. While your brain may have hundreds of different kinds of neurons arranged in a type of a web with over 100 trillion synapses, ANNs, so far, only have a handful of different kinds of neurons arranged in a layered formation, and have, at most, a few hundred million artificial synapses.

Machine learning algorithms, including ANNs, learn in the following two ways:

- **Supervised learning**: This method of learning allows the machine to learn by example. The computer is shown numerous input-output pairs, and it learns how to map input to output, even if it has never seen a certain input before. Since supervised learning systems require input and output to learn mappings, it's typically more difficult to collect data for these systems. If you'd like to train a supervised learning system to detect cats and dogs in photos, you'd need to have massive, hand-labeled datasets of images of cats and dogs and train the algorithm.
- **Unsupervised learning**: This method of learning allows the machine to learn entirely on its own. It's only shown a certain set of data, and tries to learn representations that fit the data, and can then represent new data that it has never seen before. Due to the fact that only input data is required, the method of data collection for unsupervised learning is typically easier. You'll see some examples toward the end of the book.

You can also combine these methods into a semi-supervised machine learning method, but it depends on the individual use case.

Machine learning and its uses

The machine learning technology surrounds our everyday lives, even when we don't realize it. In the following section, we can see a few examples of how ML makes our everyday lives easier:

- **Netflix:** Whenever you watch a certain show on Netflix, it's constantly learning about you, your profile, and the types of shows you like to watch. Out of its database of available movies and shows, it can recommend certain ones that it practically knows that you're going to like.

- **Amazon:** Right as you view, search for, or buy a product, Amazon's open source DSSTNE **AI** is tracking you, and will try to recommend new products that you may want to buy. Plus, it won't just recommend similar products that are in the same category or by the same brand, but it'll get down to the intricate details in suggesting those products to you, such as what others bought after viewing this product, and the specifications of those products.
- **Siri:** Nowadays, Apple's Siri isn't just a personal assistant; it analyzes practically everything you do on your phone to make your life more efficient. It'll recommend apps that you may want to launch right on the lock screen, Face ID enables 3D facial recognition in an instant on the Neural Engine (mobile neural network ASIC); and Siri shortcuts will now predict applications that you may want to open, or other media that you may want to take a look at.
- **Tesla Autopilot:** When you get on the highway in your Tesla car, your hands are probably no longer on the steering wheel, because you let autopilot take over. Using AI, your car is able to drive itself more safely than any other human ever could, by maintaining a specific preset distance between your car and the next.

Cons of machine learning

The big bad machine is taking over! This is simply untrue. In fact, this is why IBM doesn't talk about this tech as artificial intelligence but rather as augmented intelligence. It's a method of computing that extends our cognitive ability, and enhances our reasoning capabilities, whereas artificial intelligence sounds a lot more like a true, simulated intelligence.

 Whenever the term AI is used in this book, we're referring to augmented intelligence, unless otherwise stated.

There are two reasons why the majority of people believe that machine learning is here to take over humanity: namely, due to bias, and lack of understanding.

The bare-bones principles of AI have existed for long before most of us were even born. However, even as those principles came about, and before we truly understood what AI can and can't do, people started writing books and producing movies about computers taking over (for example, The **Terminator**, **HAL**, and more). This is the bias piece, which makes it hard for people to take out of their minds before they look at the reality of the technology—what machines can and cannot do from an architectural standpoint in the first place.

Also from the surface, AI looks like a very complex technology. All the mathematics and algorithms that go behind it look like a magical black box to most people. Because of this lack of understanding, people succumb to the aforementioned bias.

The primary fear that the general public has of AI is certainly the singularity, which is the point of no return, wherein AI becomes self-aware, conscious in a way and so intelligent that it's able to transcend to another level in which we can't understand what it does or why it does it. However, with the current fundamentals of computing itself, this result is simply impossible. Let's see why this is impossible with the following example.

Even as humans, we technically aren't conscious; it's only an illusion created by the very complex way our brain processes, saves, and refers back to information. Take this example: we all think that we process information by perceiving it. We look at an object and consciously perceive it, and that perception allows us or our consciousness to process it. However, this isn't true.

Let's say that we have a blind person with us. We ask them *Are you blind?*, and of course they'd say *Yes*, since they can consciously perceive that, and because they can't see. So far, this fits the hypothesis that most people have, as stated previously.

However, let's say we have a blind person with Anton-Babinski syndrome and we ask them *Are you blind?* and they affirm that they can see. Then we ask them *How many fingers am I holding up?* and they then reply with a random number. We ask them why they replied with that random number, and they then confabulate a response. Seems weird, doesn't it?

The question that arises is this: if the person can consciously realize that they can't see, then why don't they realize they're blind? There are some theories, the prevailing one stating that the visual input center of the brain isn't telling the rest of the brain anything at all. It's not even telling the brain that there is no visual input! Because of this, the rest of the neural network in the brain gets confused. This proves that there's a separation, a clear distinction, between the part of the brain that deals with the processing of information, and the part that deals with the conscious perception of that information—or, at least, forms that illusion of perception.

We can learn more on the Anton-Babinski syndrome at the following link: (`https://en.wikipedia.org/wiki/Anton%E2%80%93Babinski_syndrome`).

And here's a link to a YouTube video from *Vsauce* that talks about consciousness and what it truly is: (`https://www.youtube.com/watch?v=qjfaoe847qQ`).

And, of course, the entire *Vsauce LEANBACK*: (`https://www.youtube.com/watch?v=JoR0bMohcNo&list=PLE3048008DAA29B0A`).

There's even more evidence that hints toward the fact that consciousness isn't truly what we think of it: the theory of mind.

You may have heard of Koko the Gorilla. She was trained on sign language, so she could communicate with humans. However, researchers noticed something very interesting in Koko and other animals that were trained to communicate with humans: they don't ask questions.

This is mostly because animals don't have a theory of mind—while they may be self-aware, they aren't aware of the awareness: they aren't meta-cognizant. They don't realize that others also have a separate awareness and mind. This is an ability that, so far, we've only seen in humans.

In fact, some very young humans who are under four years old don't display this **theory of mind**. It's usually tested with the Sally-Anne test. It goes a little something like this:

1. The child is shown two dolls. Their names are Sally and Anne.
2. Sally and Anne are in a room. Sally has a basket, and Anne has a box.
3. Sally has a marble, and she puts it in the basket.
4. Sally goes for a walk outside.
5. Anne takes the marble from Sally's basket, and puts it in her own box.
6. Sally comes back from her walk, and she wants her marble. Where would Sally look for it?

If the child answers with **the box**, then they don't have that theory of mind. They don't realize that Sally and Anne (the dolls in this case) have separate minds, points of view. If they answer with **the basket**, then they realize that Sally doesn't know that Anne moved the marble from the basket to the box; they have a theory of mind.

When you put all of this together, it really starts to seem that consciousness, in the way that we think about it, really doesn't exist. It only exists as an extremely complex illusion put together by various factors, including memory and sense of time, language, self-awareness, and infinitely recursive meta-cognition, which is basically thinking about the thought itself, in an infinite loop.

To add on top of that, we don't understand how our brains are able to piece together such complex illusions in the first place. We also have to realize that any problems that we face with classical computing, due to the very fundamentals of computing itself, will apply here as well. We're dealing with math - not fundamental quantum information. Math is a human construct, built to understand, formally recognize, agree upon, and communicate the rules of the universe we live in. Realizing this, if we were to write down every single mathematical operation behind an ANN, and over the process of decades, go through the results manually on paper, would you consider the paper, the pen, or the calculator, conscious? We'd say not! So then, why would we consider an accelerated version of this, on the computer, as conscious, or being capable of self-awareness?

There is one completely rational fear of machine learning though, that humans themselves will train the computer to do negative things. This is true and it will happen. There is no way to regulate the usage of this technology. It's a set of math or an algorithm and if you ban the usage of it, someone will just implement it from scratch and use their own implementation. It's like banning the usage and purchase of guns, swords, or fire, but then, people will build their own. It's just that building a gun may be very difficult, but building AI is relatively easier, thanks to the vast amount of source code, research papers, and more that have already been published on the internet.

However, we have to trust that, similar to all other technologies that humans have developed, ML will be used for good, bad, and to prevent people from using it for bad as well. People will use ML to create cyber threats that disguise themselves from anti-viruses, but then AI systems can detect those cyber threats in turn, by using ML.

We've seen that people have used and will continue to use ML to create fake videos of people doing whatever they want them to. For example, start-ups like Lyrebird create fake audio, and other startups create fake videos of Barack Obama saying anything they want him to say. However, there are still very subtle patterns that let us detect whether a video is real or fake patterns that humans and conventional algorithms simply cannot detect, but ML technology can.

Introduction to IBM Watson

If what you've read so far piques your interest, then welcome aboard! For, in this book, you won't be learning the actual, raw algorithms that go behind the tech. Rather, you'll be getting a much simpler introduction to the world of AI—through IBM Watson.

Watson, in this context, is a set of REST APIs that are available in the IBM Cloud that enables you to create cognitive applications, without the complex, expensive, and long process of developing cognitive from scratch. But there's more!

Let's begin!

Hardware and software requirements

Now, let's talk about how you can set up your environment to work with ML technology.

One of the key aspects to using a cloud-based service, such as Watson, is that you don't need to own any of the intense hardware that usually goes behind deep learning, or machine learning, systems. Everything's done in the cloud for you, and it is billed based on how much of, or how long, you use the services and machines for.

Therefore, there are no strict hardware requirements.

This book will deal mainly with Python 3.7.2, so it's preferable to have a POSIX-compliant (Unix-like) OS, but Windows will also work, preferably **Windows Subsystem for Linux** (**WSL**).

Signing up for IBM Cloud

Now that you're ready, let's sign up for IBM Cloud. To begin with, you don't have to pay for IBM Cloud, or even provide your credit card information. Using the **IBM Cloud Lite** tier, you can use most services for free!

While it is quite self-explanatory, here's a list of steps to sign up for IBM Cloud:

1. Head over to `https://www.ibm.com/cloud`
2. Hit the **Sign up for IBM Cloud** button
3. Fill in all the required information
4. Verify your email address by clicking the link sent to your email
5. Once you're in IBM Cloud, give a name to your brand new space and organization

An organization is a set of spaces relevant to a certain company or entity, and a space is a set of services or applications relevant to a project.

Summary

There we go—once you've created an IBM Cloud account, you should be ready for the next steps. After completing this chapter, you should be able to understand what machine learning is and how it can be used to make use of gold mines of structured and unstructured data that, so far, were deemed useless. We have also learned about the limitations of conventional computing and machine learning. We got a basic understanding of what IBM Watson is and what the necessary hardware and software requirement's are and we learned how to sign up for IBM Cloud.

In the next chapter, we will learn how to apply machine learning through IBM Watson.

2
Can Machines Converse Like Humans?

We are exposed to a wide range of chatbots in our everyday activities—Siri, Alexa, and Google Home are just a few examples. I can speak out loud to various devices with utterances, such as, *Siri, what is the weather in Seattle?* or *Alexa, Turn on the lights*, or *Google, What is the tallest mountain in the world?* And these devices just respond with answers or actions.

What they do is fairly remarkable in that there are many ways of inquiring about the weather. For example, I might say, *What is the weather in Washington?*, *Tell me the temperature in Seattle*, or even the more ambiguous, *What is it like up North?* All of these have essentially the same intent and are generally referring to the same location. For the most part, all of these devices are doing the same thing: using machine learning algorithms to classify your intention, and to determine the entity (location, in this case) you are inquiring about. They then need to map that onto some predefined action, such as determining the weather, switching on the lights in your room, or looking up some information. There is no doubt that doing these basic activities in response to your vocal expression is useful. However, these really are not conversations. They are simple single-turn command-response, or question-response systems. What they fail to do is to get to the heart of the problem, which is how we distinguish them from conversational agents.

If I ask a service agent, *What is my account balance?* I need to know what my balance is. But that's not really my problem. My bigger concern is that I'm getting ready to buy something, or I'm trying save up for my kid's education, or trying to pay my bills. There is something deeper and more important to me than simply trying to see how much money I have. A conversation is about trying to get to that deeper concern.

A conversation between two people generally involves each person coming into the conversation with their own set of ideas. Over the course of the discussion, those ideas are expressed, reshaped, or reinforced; they're blended in some way. The result is that each person goes away from any conversation with something they didn't have when they went in. A problem is solved, new ideas are created, or new issues revealed. The conversation is a catalyst in the creative process. And that's the effect that we are looking for in conversational agents, and what distinguishes them from the plethora of chatbots on the market today.

But, is that possible from **artificial intelligence** (**AI**)? What are the means by which AI is able to both assist people in uncovering their problems, and inspire them with new ideas that will help them solve those problems better than they could on their own? Certainly, that requires something more than a simple chatbot. Fortunately, for most deployments of AI in useful scenarios, the context of its use has a naturally limiting scope—that is, if you're working with a bank, conversations are likely to be confined to banking concerns; if you're dealing with a retail store, they are likely to be oriented to issues having to do with finding products, or getting problems with those products resolved. This both helps in the construction of an effective conversational agent, and also corresponds nicely to real-world experiences. You generally don't make an appointment to see your doctor to discuss real estate questions; you don't stop random people on the street to converse about that rash that has been creeping up your leg. The context of the conversation generally determines the kinds of things that we will discuss in that conversation. Knowing this will help simplify the task of creating a great conversational agent.

In this chapter, we will help you understand how to build a conversational agent—first by creating a workspace in which to build and train your conversation service, and then showing you how to program an application to use that workspace.

We will cover the following topics in this chapter:

- Creating a conversational agent workspace
- Creating a set of conversational intents
- Programming your conversational application

Creating a conversational agent workspace

Like nearly all of the Watson-branded offerings, the Watson Assistant is an **application programming interface (API)** hosted in the IBM Cloud. You learned how to create an account in the IBM Cloud in *Chapter 1*, *Background, Transition, and the Future of Computing*. We'll pick up from there by guiding you through the creation of an instance of the Watson Assistant service—referred to as a workspace—in which you will customize and train the service to your conversational context.

Creating an instance of Watson Assistant and a workspace

To get started, we need to create a workspace that Watson can work with:

1. After creating an account, go to the IBM Cloud services catalog at `https://console.bluemix.net/catalog/`. Be sure that you are logged in with your account—you should see your username in the upper-right corner of the browser window:

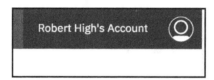

2. Otherwise, press the **Log in** button:

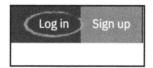

3. Select **AI** in the **All Categories** section:

4. From there, select the **Watson Assistant (formerly Conversation)** card:

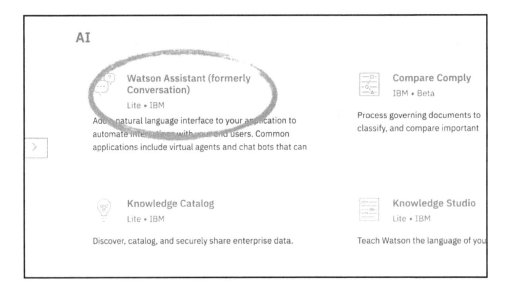

5. This will take you to a page where you can choose a region where you want to deploy the service, and select a **Pricing Plan**. For this exercise, pick a region that is closest to you, scroll down to select the **Free Lite pricing plan**, and then press the **Create** button at the bottom-right:

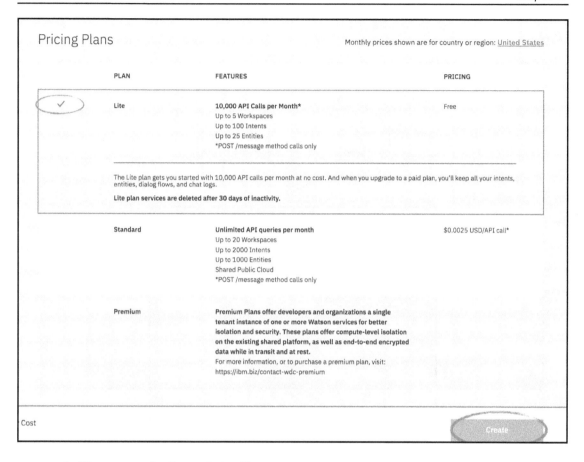

6. Then press the **Launch tool** button:

7. Select the **Workspaces** tab:

8. Then press the **Create** button:

Before going further, let's discuss the example use case and scenario that we're about to demonstrate. Follow along with us for now, but eventually we would encourage you to invent your own scenario and build a conversational agent that meets your needs.

The sample application

We will build an application to handle a set of banking activities, such as checking your account balances, transferring funds, paying a credit card bill, and so forth. We'll keep this fairly simple to begin with, and then expand on this use case as we get deeper into other topics.

The application will begin with a text interface that we can run on a web page. We will expand that further, to run as an App on your mobile phone with a voice-activated interface. The thing to realize is that, since the Watson Assistant service is a callable API, the same conversational capabilities can be included into any number of application frontends—web applications, mobile phones, text messaging, other messaging platforms, such as Twitter, WhatsApp, or WeChat, as well as embedded system devices.

Creating a set of conversational intents

The first thing we need to do is identify the set of intents we want to support in this conversational agent. An intent is just an action that the end user may express, and that we want the application to support. Identifying the set of intents is actually pretty straightforward and can be derived from virtually any existing banking web application.

This is a pretty common example of a typical set of actions you can perform on a banking application:

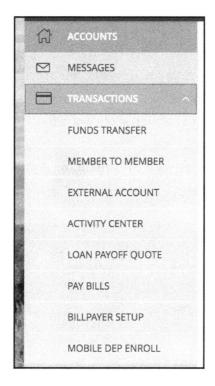

Here is the list of banking services that you might find on the Web:

- **ACCOUNTS**: Information on what accounts you have, and their balances, along with other information about the account
- **MESSAGES**: Where you would receive any notifications from the bank
- **FUNDS TRANSFER**: Enables you to move money between your own accounts
- **MEMBER TO MEMBER**: Supports transferring money from your account to someone else's account within the same banking institution
- **EXTERNAL ACCOUNT**: Enables you to link accounts that you have at other institutions
- **ACTIVITY CENTER**: Gives you a summary of the transactions that have been performed recently on your accounts
- **LOAN PAYOFF QUOTE**: Tells you how much you will need to pay off one of your loans
- **PAY BILLS**: Enables you to initiate an online bill payment
- **BILLPAYER SETUP**: Lets you set up the billing information for any bills you may want to pay online in the future
- **MOBILE DEP ENROLL**: Walks you through the steps for making online deposits to your account with your smartphone

A more complete banking application will enable you to do a number of other things, but this is a pretty good starting set.

So now, we can return to the conversation service and finish setting up the banking workspace:

Enter the name of the workspace—we'll call it **Banking Application** in this example—and then press **Create**:

We need to create a set of intents that we can derive from the set of actions that we outline above from our Banking web application.

Press the **Add intent** button:

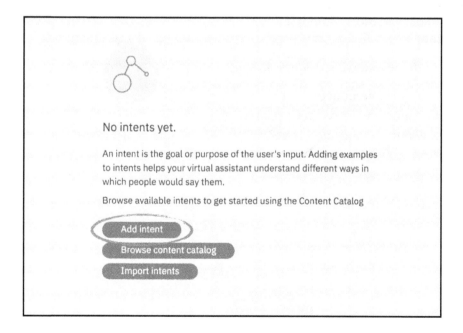

We'll add the `Accounts` intent in the **Intent name** (you don't have to prefix the name with a #—that is done automatically by the tool), and then press the **Create intent** button:

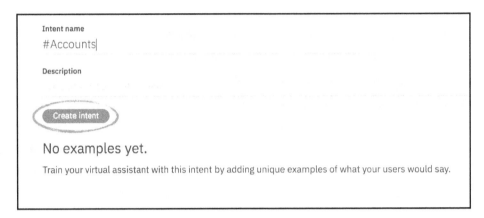

You now need to train Watson to recognize how people express this intent. Consider that people have different ways of saying things. You can certainly test yourself, using all of the different ways you can think of asking about your account balance. However, remember that, in all likelihood, whatever you think of, someone else will think of a different way to ask the same thing. It is often useful to consult recordings of what people have said in live situations, if you have access to such information. But the beauty of Watson is that it learns pretty quickly, so even just giving it a few examples will probably be enough for it to understand most variations. And if it doesn't, you can always go back later and train Watson further by providing some more examples of things it's getting wrong.

We'll begin with the following examples:

- What is my account balance?
- How much do I have in Checking?
- How much money do I have?
- What is my current balance?
- How much savings do I have?

Enter each example for the intent:

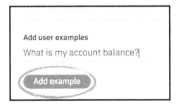

It may not be obvious, but every time you enter a new example, Watson begins training on that example. If you press the **Try it** button in the upper-right corner, you may catch Watson doing that training:

Go ahead and press the **Try it** button. That will open a side panel on the right of your window. Once Watson has completed training (which should only take a few seconds), you can enter some text at the bottom of that panel:

Try something such as **How much do I have?** If Watson has done its job properly, it should recognize that as being an #Accounts intent, and will report so in a response message that looks like this:

Actually, at this point, Watson is likely to assume just about anything you tell it that is similar to this is likely to be about the `#Accounts` intent as it hasn't been taught anything else—not until you enter examples for the other intents. For example, if you enter `What's the beef?` it's likely to think you're asking about your account balance. That said, other more extreme differences, such as `I want a Taco`, are likely to be recognized as irrelevant.

When you're done entering examples for the `#Accounts` intent, press the back-button:

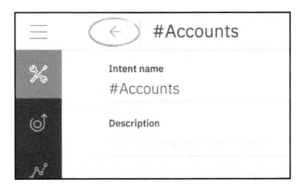

This will take you back to the main **Intents** page where you can enter the other Intents, and corresponding examples:

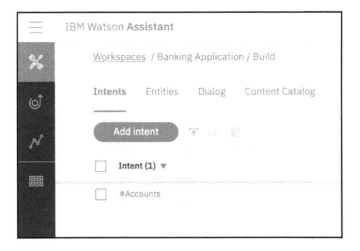

When entering an **Intent** name, it cannot contain spaces (or a number of other special characters). So for something such as `Funds Transfer` you can replace the **space** with a **dash** to look something like `Funds-Transfer`.

When you've finished, go back to the **Try it** panel and test Watson on how well it is able to understand the intent of your utterances, as in the following screenshot:

If Watson gets it wrong—for example, maybe you think the `What do I have left?` utterance expresses the intent to pay off a loan, but Watson understands it to be an `Account` inquiry:

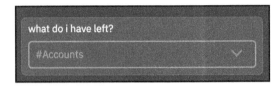

You can correct Watson by pressing the **down button** on the intent, and making it the intent you believe it should have been:

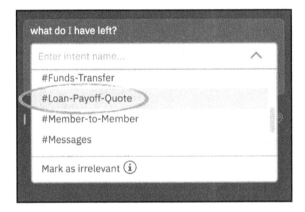

This will cause Watson to add that test example to the training data for `#Loan-Payoff-Quote`, and retrain to recognize that better in the future:

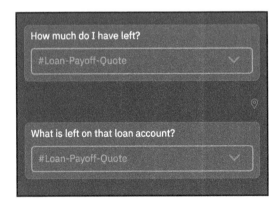

Recognizing entities

Now, let's talk about entities. In many of the examples I ended up using to train Watson, I included references to specific things. These are some examples I used:

- How much do I have in checking?
- What transactions have I done recently?
- Put money in my wife's account
- Pay my power bill

We can look at one of the preceding examples in the following screenshot:

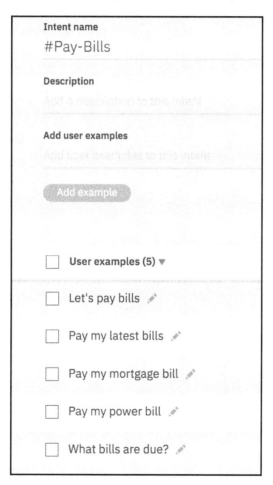

`Checking`, `I`, `recently`, `my wife`, and `my power bill` are all examples of entities that qualify my intent. I specifically want to know how much money I have in my checking account—not just any account. I want to know about transactions that I have performed recently—not those that others have performed, and certainly not those that my wife may have made a while ago (note that statements such as recently and a while ago are both relative and somewhat ambiguous timeframes, requiring a certain judgement to evaluate).

So, we have to teach Watson to recognize these types of qualifications. We call those **entities**—essentially people, places, things, and timeframes.

There are two ways to identify entities in Watson.

The first is to go back to the intent examples you have provided. Mouse over to select the thing that represents an entity, for example power bill, and create or identify the name of that entity type:

The other approach to creating entities is to go into the **Entities** tab on the main conversation page and press the **Add entity** button:

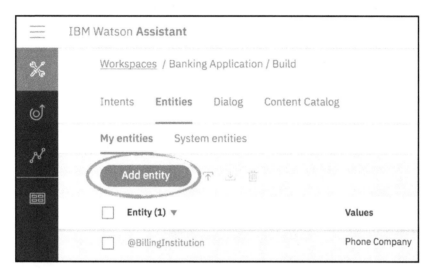

You can create an entity for `PersonalRelations`:

Then, you can add values for `Mother, Myself, Father, Daughter, Son, Husband,` and `Wife`, for example, along with any synonyms for each of those. Now add any other entities that you think will be relevant to conversations about banking activities. We depict a few other entities you can create here:

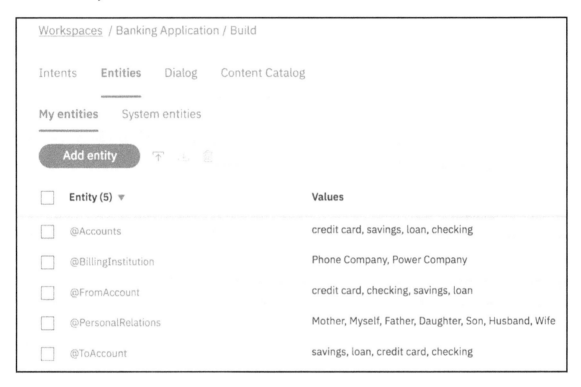

In this case, we have created entities for Accounts, in addition to `BillingInstitutions` and `PersonalRelations`. And, again, you can test this out with the **Try it** button:

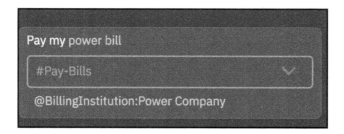

Note, that Watson recognized that I intended to `#Pay-Bills` and to do so for my `@BillingInstitution:Power Company`—identified as an entity that qualifies the intent. In addition to user-defined entities, Watson also supplies a list of predefined system entities. If you select **System entities** tab on the main **Entity** page, you will see a list of them:

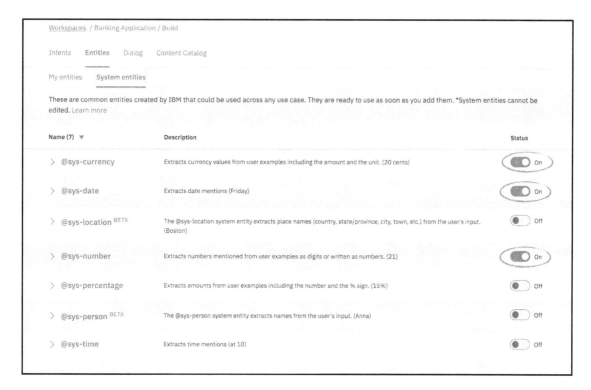

You can introduce system-defined entities into your application by simply turning them **On**.

Now we have done enough to build a very basic chatbot. We could, for example, write an application that prompted for a text utterance from a user, calling the Watson Assistant service passing in the utterance, and the service would return with a classification value and entities. You could, in your application, take that result and use it to determine the outstanding balance of the power bill, and issue a transaction to transfer that amount to the power company.

Identifying entities through annotators

Let's return to the first style of identifying an entity that you care about. In the first approach, we showed you in **Recognizing entities**, we went to the intent examples, and highlighted the entity that we cared about in that example. We refer to this as the annotator approach to entity recognition. Annotators are a much more powerful way of identifying the entities. Rather than setting a rule, such as the word *hot* is a temperature entity, the annotator approach builds a machine learning algorithm that takes in the context of the surrounding words in the sentence. In doing so, it calculates the probability that hot is referring to a temperature. In a sentence such as *The water is hot*, it makes sense to recognize **hot** as being a temperature. But in another sentence, such as *The market is hot*, it should be taken to be the relative value people place on a particular product.

As your conversational agent gets more sophisticated, you will likely want to make more use of the annotator approach to entity recognition, as doing so will make its interpretation more robust. However, keep in mind that, like most machine learning problems, you have to teach Watson through examples—generally with several examples. If you're going to use this approach, you should find several examples in your intent training set in which you make use of the different entity types you care about, and label them accordingly.

So, in this example, we have added a few examples of the #Funds-Transfer intent, and, within that we have annotated, (as indicated by their highlights in the following example) a number of @Account entities:

← #Funds-Transfer

#Funds-Transfer

Description

Add user examples

Add example

☐ User examples (15) ▼

☐ Can you transfer bewteen my credit card and savings

☐ Deposit $200 to checking

☐ Deposit to another account

☐ give me some dough

☐ I want to move some money

☐ Move money between accounts

☐ Move money from checking to savings

☐ Move to my Checking account

☐ Put $200 into my savings, from my loan account

☐ Take $100 from savings and put into checking

☐ Transfer funds

☐ Transfer money

☐ Transfer money from savings

Building a dialog

To make your application a little more interesting, you can preface the interaction with a little greeting, and some sort of acknowledgement. We'll do that now.

You can introduce a dialog by pressing the **Dialog** tab of the main workspace screen and press the **Create** button. This will begin with a very basic dialog flow already filled out for you—including what to say to get things going, and how to respond in the case the user utters something completely off-topic:

Press on the **Welcome** card and an edit screen will come up on the right. You can modify the text that Watson will respond with, for example, change it to `Welcome to ABC Bank. What can I do for you?`:

Now, let's provide an interesting response if the user wants to pay their power bill. Press the **Add node** button, and in the **If bot recognizes:** field enter `#Pay-Bills`, press the + sign to the right of that, and enter `@BillingInstitution:(Phone Company)` in the field that opens up. There are auto-complete prompts for each of these steps that will help you fill in the values. Finally, enter `Thank-you, we will pay your Power Bill` in the **Then respond with:** field:

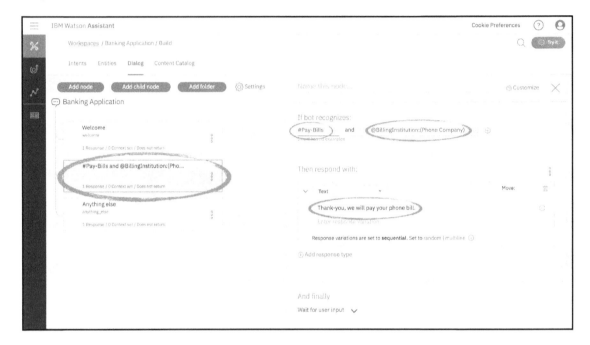

Now, let's try it out. You should see the following:

Of course, what you're seeing in the preceding **Try it out** screen is a prototype application that is exercising the dialog you just created along with the intents and entities that you've trained Watson to recognize. In your own application, you will be able to build the user interface to suit whatever is appropriate for your audience.

Creating the dialog for a complex Intent using Frame Slots

Now let's examine a slightly more complex case. In the **Try it** out panel, enter Transfer money to my mother's savings account. You should see it come back with something like this:

In this case, Watson has recognized the intent to transfer money to my mother's account. Again, we can imagine the application resolving who my mother is by looking up my account relationship information—perhaps that is an account that I had previously identified as a linked account. However, as straightforward as this little interaction seems, it might be somewhat unsatisfying for the end user. After all, how much does the user want to transfer, and from what account should the transfer be made?

To make this more complete, we need to do a bit more work.

In this case, we're going to create what we call a frame-slot dialog. That is, a dialog whose goal is to fill in all the information needed to complete the transaction. We'll use the #Funds-Transfer intent to demonstrate this. Transferring money between accounts depends on three things: the amount to transfer, where to take it from, and where to put it. We'll show you how to add this additional level of sophistication now.

We will begin adding another node to the dialog. Press the **Add node** button on the **Dialog** pane:

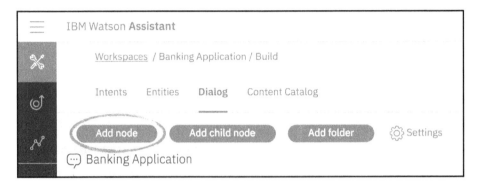

In the edit window, you can set this node to look for #Fund-Transfer, and then press the **Customize** button:

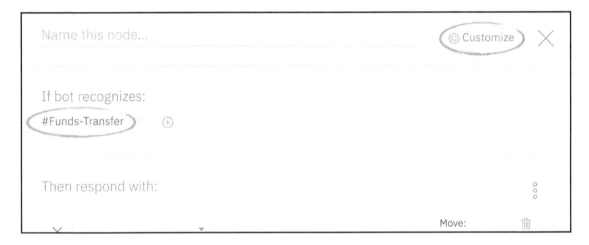

Pressing **Customize** will bring up a dialog box, where you can turn on and apply slot-processing for this node:

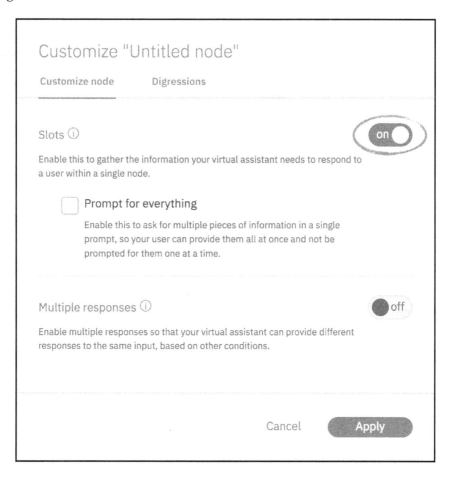

This will open the dialog node to a set of slots, and we can begin by creating a slot for gathering the from account information. Fill in @Accounts in the Check for field, $FromAccount in the **Save** it as field, and What account do you want to debit? in the **If not present, ask** field:

Context variables

Before we go further, we need to discuss context variables. Any robust conversational agent will benefit from context. Context enables memory between turns in the conversation and enables anaphora—reducing the awkward need to repeat words, especially nouns, used earlier in the exchange. Context is represented within the dialog as a set of developer-defined context variables, represented with the $ prefix, and passed between the application and the conversation service through a JSON structure.

Keep in mind that the Watson Assistant conversational API is stateless—that is, it doesn't maintain any memory of prior calls to the service, and therefore any state, such as context, must be passed back and forth between your application and the service. This will become more obvious when we show how your application can call the service API, later in this chapter.

In the preceding example, the dialog node will check for the existence of the `@Accounts` entity in the user's utterance. If it finds it, the value of the `@Accounts` entity will be assigned to the `$FromAccount` context variable.

If that slot `@Accounts` entity is not found, the dialog node will prompt the user with the `What account do you want to debit?` question, all of which you will enter into the slot fields. Let's try it out.

Enter transfer funds in the **Try it out** tool:

Notice, that Watson recognized that the utterance is intended to mean #Funds-Transfer, and that it didn't find any @Accounts entities, so it prompted for it. You can now respond to that with savings. Watson realized that you are still responding to the #Funds-Transfer intent, and that you expressed an @Accounts entity of savings:

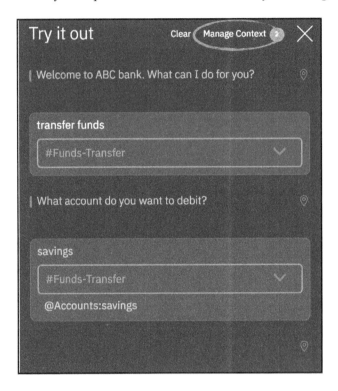

Now, if you press the **Manage Context** button at the top of the panel, you will see that the $FromAccount context variable was filled in. The $timezone context variable is always filled in automatically by Watson:

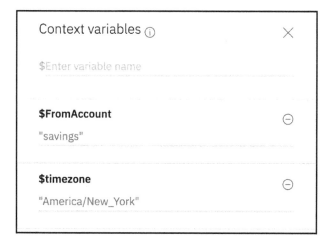

Now, we can return to editing the dialog node to create slots for the target account and amount to transfer:

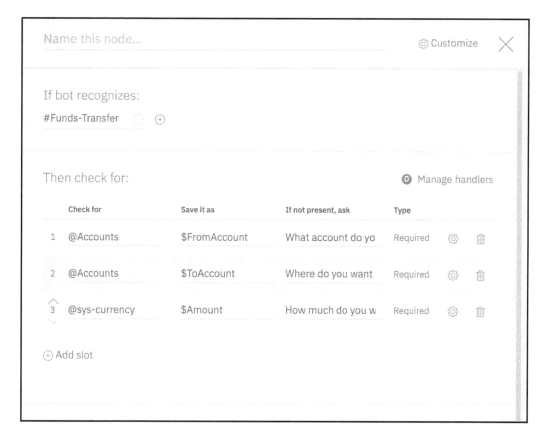

The same entity type is sought to fill in the $FromAccount and $ToAccount context variables. Watson is smart enough to realize these should represent two different instances of the @Accounts entity.

We can finish out the node by instructing Watson to acknowledge the transfer by filling in the **Then respond with:** field of the node with something such as Thank you. We will transfer $$Amount from $FromAccount to $ToAccount:

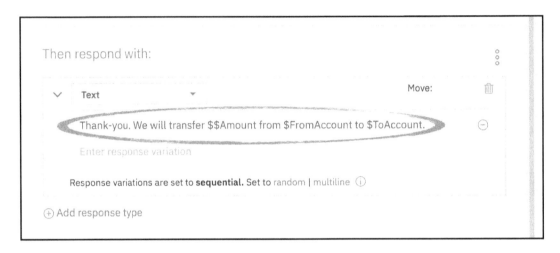

We can then try it out in various ways, as follows:

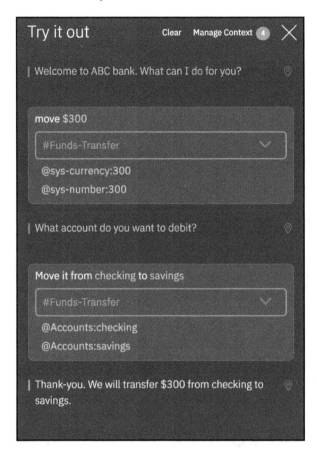

You can fill in multiple slots with the same utterance.

While Watson remains quite robust with this simple example—able to understand your intent even when expressed in a variety of different ways—it's also not entirely infallible. For example, if you reverse the `from` and `to` accounts in your expression, as follows, Watson can get confused:

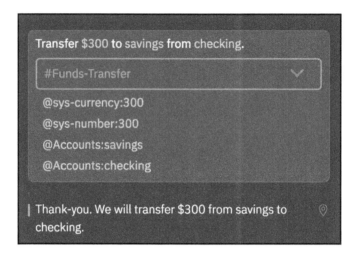

However, the Watson tooling is quite sophisticated. There are a variety of techniques that can be used to overcome this type of confusion. We won't go into the details at this time, but we do encourage you to explore the tooling and the wide range of educational materials posted on the Web to learn more.

Programming your conversation application

So, now we're ready to start developing an application to make use of your trained Watson conversation. For this, we're going to use Python, and we're less concerned with the proper structuring of the application as a whole than with the structuring of your calls to the Watson Assistant services. However, before we begin, we need to get the Python SDK for Watson. If you don't already have Python installed, go to `https://www.python.org/`.

Once you have Python installed, you should be able to use the PIP tool to download and install the Watson SDK by issuing the following command in a terminal window:

```
pip install --upgrade ibm-watson
```

There are occasions where you may run into permission errors when you issue that command on Mac or Linux. If you do, type the following command:

```
sudo -H pip install --ignore-installed six ibm-watson
```

More information about the **software developer kit** (**SDK**) can be found at `https:// github.com/watson-developer-cloud/python-sdk`. The Watson developer SDKs (for a variety of programming languages) make it convenient and very easy to invoke Watson services from your laptop, smartphone, a server, another Cloud—virtually anywhere you want to run your application.

You will also need to install other dependencies as described in: `https://github.com/ watson-developer-cloud/python-sdk#dependencies`.

The first thing you will need to do in your program is to import the `ibm_watson` library, like this:

```
import ibm_watson
```

Of course, you may want to import other libraries that will be useful to your application, such as the `json` library.

You will then create a session with the Watson Assistant service you created earlier in this chapter. The code for that looks like this:

[Chp2-Program-1.py]

```
assistant = ibm_watson.AssistantV1(
        iam_apikey='PrLJLVykZG4V-FQrADLiZG91oOKcJN0UZWEUAo0HxW8Q',
        version='2018-09-20')
```

You will get the apikey value from the **Credentials** page for the service. You can get to them by pressing the **Deploy** (looks like a circular arrow) button to the left of the conversation editor:

This will bring up the **Deploy** page. You can then press the **Credentials** tab:

The **Username** and **Password** are listed on the page, like this:

Just copy and paste the values from the screen into your program.

The version is provided to you as part of the API specification, which you can find at `https://www.ibm.com/watson/developercloud/assistant/api/v1/python.html? python#introduction`.

Once you have the session established, you can go on to call the Watson Assistant service, like this:

[Chp2-Program-2.py]

```
response = assistant.message(
       workspace_id='3e86c7a1-b071-4e6a-ada2-a8ac616e6aa6'
    ).get_result()
```

`workspace_id` is the identity of the specific conversation workspace that you have created. Again, you can do that from the **Deploy Credentials** page, as seen in the following screenshot:

As before, just cut and paste the **Workspace ID** value into your application.

We should also take a moment to explain what else is going on in this piece of code. We're making a call to the `message()` function on the `AssistantV1` class instance that we created when we opened a session to the Watson Assistant. We're passing in the workspace ID that we want to operate on, and we're getting back a response that we retrieve with the `get_result()` function.

The response is a JSON structure returned by the service and we can use standard Python JSON operations to parse.

If you want to visually examine the contents of the returned response, you use the `json.dumps()` function within a `print()` statement, as follows. This will print out the JSON contents in a readable form:

```
print(json.dumps(response, indent=2))
```

We can make this call to Watson without the benefit of any input from the user. To do this the first time, typically, we prompt Watson for whatever greeting was established to open the conversation.

Remember the **Welcome** node in your dialog that we created earlier in this chapter? It looked something like the following:

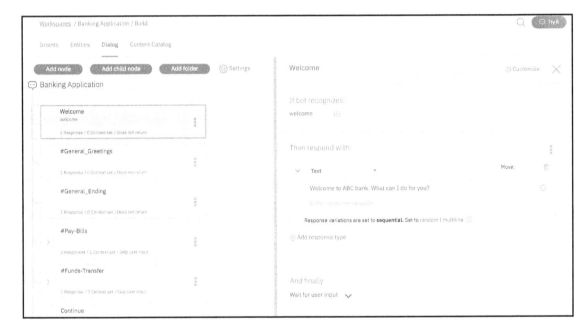

The **Welcome** node describes the opening text of your dialog. Having retrieved it from Watson, you can now present it to the user to prompt them for input, and subsequently request their input. Having got their input utterance, you can then submit that back to Watson for further processing—perhaps in a loop that goes back and forth between the following:

- Requesting input from the user
- Processing that with Waston
- Presenting the response from Watson back to the user

This will continue until the conversation terminates in a graceful manner.

The call to Watson within this loop might look more like the following:

```
[Chp2-Program-2.py]

response = assistant.message(
        workspace_id='3e86c7a1-b071-4e6a-ada2-a8ac616e6aa6',
        input={'text': utterance}, context=response.get("context")
    ).get_result()
```

As before, we are supplying the `workspace_id`, but this time we're supplying two other parameters: the user's utterance, which is supplied as a **JavaScript object notation** (**JSON**) input string, and the context retrieved from the prior call to Watson—the latter is needed to retain some fluidity between each interaction with Watson.

A more complete example application might look like the following:

```python
import json
import ibm_watson

def BankBot():

    # Create session with the Watson Assistant
    assistant = ibm_watson.AssistantV1(
            iam_apikey='PrLJLVykZG4V-FQrADLiZG91oOKcJN0UZWEUAo0HxW8Q',
            version='2018-09-20')

    # Pull the first prompt from the Dialog
    response = assistant.message(
            workspace_id='3e86c7a1-b071-4e6a-ada2-a8ac616e6aa6').get_result()

    # Continue prompting the user and getting their input, until they indicate
    # it's time to quit
    while True:

        # Get the text of the prompt
        prompt = response.get('output').get('text')

        # Display all of the text provided in the prompt
        for text in prompt:
            print(text)

        # Get the user's next utterance
        utterance = input("==> ")

        # Invoke Watson to assess the intent of the utterance and determine how
        # to respond to the user
        response = assistant.message(
                workspace_id='3e86c7a1-b071-4e6a-ada2-a8ac616e6aa6',
                input={'text': utterance},
                context=response.get('context')
            ).get_result()

        # Ensure there are intents in the response.
        if len(response.get("intents")) > 0:

            #Check whether the dialog indicates an end to the conversation
            if response["intents"][0]["intent"] == "General_Ending":
                if len(response.get("output").get("text")) > 0:
                    # If there are any remaining messages in the response then
                    # print them out.
                    print(response.get("output").get("text")[0] + '\n')
                    # And terminate the conversation.
                    break

        # If there are other intents that need processing, that logic can
        # go here


BankBot()
```

We call this function `BankBot()`. Let's examine it in more detail:

- On line 7 we are creating the session to Watson Assistant.
- On line 12 we call the assistant to get its opening statement.
- We go into a loop on line 17.
- On line 20 we are getting the text that Watson would have us present to the user.
- Keep in mind that Watson may have us present multiple lines of text, so, on line 23, we are printing however many lines of text Watson has given us.
- On line 27, we prompt the user for their utterance, which we pass back into Watson on line 31, along with the context from the prior invocation of Watson.
- On line 38, we check whether Watson has decided to terminate the conversation (generally due to something the user said)—in this case by looking for the `General_Ending` intent.
- If this is the end of the conversation, we check whether there are any last things Watson would have us tell the user—usually a salutation of some sort—and then we break out of the loop on line 47.

This may result in a conversation that looks something like this:

```
Welcome to ABC bank. What can I do for you?
==> i want to transfer some money from my checking account
How much do you want to transfer?
==> $250
Where do you want to deposit?
==> put it in savings
Thank-you. We will transfer $250 from checking to savings.

What else can I help you with?
==> I want to pay off my credit card
Thank-you, we will pay your credit card.

Is there anything else you need?
==> no, that will do, thanks
Thank-you for letting us help you.
```

More typically, your application will get involved in the conversation by acting on various intents, such as performing the actual transfer of funds or leveraging an existing backend transaction system. That logic might typically be inserted at the same point where other checks, such as ending the conversation, are being performed.

Emerging features

As we write this, IBM is developing some enhancements to the Watson Assistant service that will be available by the time this book is published. These include introducing the formal concept of an assistant. In essence, an assistant represents the persona facing your user set. Often an enterprise will give their virtual assistant a name – it's essentially an extension of their company brand. The assistant concept within the service serves as an aggregation point for the things that enable the brand's identity.

Generally, an assistant has a Skill—a formal reference to the set of Intents, Entities, and Dialogs that you created in your workspace. Any assistant you create is said to have that skill. But this formalism also makes deploying your assistant easier too. For example, having created an assistant, given it a name, and associated its Skill set, the Watson Assistant tooling makes it very easy to deploy that assistant through a variety of messaging platforms, such as Facebook Messenger, Slack, or Intercom. You can initiate that by pressing the **Add Integration** button on the **Assistant** tab:

This will take you to a page that offers a variety of automated and manual integration choices to help you simplify your integration.

Summary

In this chapter, you learned about the Watson Assistant service. A good conversational agent is more than a single-turn, transactional response system. A conversation is about getting to the heart of the user's problem—keeping in mind that the first question someone asks is often not the question they really want to ask. Sometimes they don't even know what question to ask to solve their problem—they need to be walked through it. We've taught you the fundamentals of how to create a workspace in which you can train Watson to recognize the intents that your users might express, and to extract the entities within that expression. We also looked at how to build a dialog flow, in which you can guide the user through their conversation. We showed you how to jump around within that flow to address different ways that a user might proceed with their side of the conversation. Finally, we explained how to write a program in Python to make use of the service and from which you can drive the interaction with your end users.

In the next chapter, we will discuss Watson's Visual Recognition service, and how that can be used to classify different objects in a photograph or video image. We will elaborate on ways the Visual Recognition service can be used to characterize what it finds in those images.

Further reading

There are many tutorials and advanced-topic assets that you can use to learn more about the content covered in this chapter. Here are some of our favorites:

- Getting Chatty with IBM Watson by Simon Burns: `https://medium.com/ @snrubnomis/getting-chatty-with-ibm-watson-1075c549ee9e`
- Conversation Patterns with IBM Watson by Simon Burns: `https://medium.com/ @snrubnomis/conversation-patterns-with-ibm-watson-6c4be05e2fe5`
- Solution Tutorials: `https://console.bluemix.net/docs/tutorials/index. html#tutorials`

3
Computer Vision

Welcome to the third chapter in your journey into the world of Watson. In this chapter, you're going to learn about computer vision! In doing so, you're also going to learn a lot more about the underlying visual systems in animals, how and why computer vision evolved, and why understanding visual data is so complex. I'll then walk you through how you can implement computer vision with Watson; we'll do this with both custom datasets and some pre-trained classifiers from Watson, such as those for facial detection.

In this chapter, we will cover the following topics:

- Can machines visually perceive the world around them?
- Uploading data and training the classifier
- Creating a Python application to classify with Watson

Can machines visually perceive the world around them?

Although primitive at the time, the sense of sight evolved in animals around 700,000,000 years ago. As humans, it's our primary sense, and around half of all of our mental processing power at any given time goes to visual perception—you may have realized this about your dreams, too!

While it may seem very simple, our sense of sight is actually a lot more complex than we thought! As humans, we gain a great understanding of the world around us through our sense of sight.

What's really interesting, however, is how we humans can recognize the objects around us. For example, if you were to look at a car, how does your brain know that you're looking at a car, and therefore create a conscious perception of a **car**?

It seems like a simple question, but the amount of learning and logic that goes into recognizing objects is truly remarkable. Even more noteworthy is that we can recognize objects with very little data, as well! Say you were shown a lawnmower and a snowblower for the first time in your life. If you were shown another snowblower, you'd instantly recognize it as a snowblower despite having only seen one other snowblower in your life.

Machines have, traditionally, had a very hard time understanding visual data—which is data presented in the form of images. This is due to the large number of ways a single entity can be represented. For example, you could take a picture of a golden retriever in your backyard or a husky in a parking lot, and both of the images represent a dog. However, for a computer, there isn't even any immediate discernible similarity in the pixels between those images that would tell you they both contain a dog—let alone the breed of said dog. With a computer, you can trace the path of individual photons, which is called ray-tracing, to render a near-real-life-quality scene in near-real-time, which is unfathomably computationally expensive. However, you can't tell whether the image you just took contains a cat, a dog, or a truck!

This is where Machine Learning comes in. Older techniques, such as feature engineering, have almost all been replaced by newer techniques, such as Deep Learning. All you'd need to do as a programmer is provide two things: preprocessed training data and a neural network architecture to train and re-train. Luckily, Watson takes care of the neural network part *and* the preprocessing for training data, which means that you just need to provide the raw training data.

Responsibility then:	You	You	You
Tasks:	Data collection	Data preprocessing	Neural network architecture for training
Responsibility now:	You	Watson	Watson

The past – classical computer vision

In the past, programmers would go through a painstaking and long process to create computer vision algorithms that were, well, less than satisfactory. This process was called **feature engineering**.

Essentially, you'd manually design **features** or **filters** that would act as filters on an image, and if an image is activated above a certain threshold by certain, handcrafted filters, it would be given a certain class.

This technique is not very scalable, takes a very long time, takes smart people, and doesn't provide very good accuracy, at least by today's standards.

The present – deep learning for computer vision

Nowadays, deep neural networks (also called **Deep Learning algorithms**) have mostly replaced feature engineering. With Deep Learning, the computer does the feature engineering for you by finding patterns in the images themselves.

Convolutional neural networks in particular are used for anything to do with visual data, such as image classification or image regression. They're derived from the Neocognitron, developed by Professor Fukushima in 1980—a kind of neural network that's tolerant to shifts and deformation. For example, if you were to write the letter 6 a few pixels to the left or right, it's still a 6.

In a convolutional neural network, there are convolutional layers that are stacked one on top of another. The input to the first layer is, of course, the input image. The layer will take several learned features and run them as filters on the image. These filtered versions of the image will be fed into the next layer, which will use features to further filter the image, and so on and so forth.

Of course, it's a bit more complex than that; there are other layers, such as pooling (reducing the size of the images) and activation layers (to regularize the data).

However, since the neural network learns the filters on its own, it's able to do some neat things; for example, when you train a neural network to classify, say, faces, it'll learn the following features:

- The first layer will recognize very simple patterns, such as edges and lines.
- The next few layers will recognize slightly more complex, but still simple, patterns such as curves and simple shapes.
- The next few layers will learn more abstract patterns, such as combining those curves and shapes to reconstruct eyes, mouths, and noses.
- The last few layers will learn how to combine those abstract patterns into full faces.
- A feed-forward neural network will be used to classify the final features extracted by the convolutional neural network.

This is just an example—since the computer is learning on its own, it'll figure out what each layer learns. However, it does convey this: with every layer, the computer learns continuously more advanced and abstract patterns.

This opens up an interesting possibility: if you were to train a convolutional neural network to recognize cats and dogs, could you use the features it has already learned in order to train another neural network to recognize, say, lions and cheetahs? That's what transfer learning aims to achieve.

With transfer learning, since you're learning from a pre-trained neural network, you won't need as much data to train the neural network. Simple patterns have already been defined—you only need to fine-tune the more abstract ones.

This is one of the techniques used by Watson Visual Recognition in order to classify images based off of very little data.

Of course, there are other techniques used to help Watson, such as data augmentation, but we won't be getting deeper into that in this book.

Creating a basic image-recognition system

Just like with the Watson Assistant, the Watson Visual Recognition service is an API hosted in the IBM Cloud. However, the tooling or GUI for the Visual Recognition service is located within the Watson Studio interface. In this book, we won't be covering the Watson Studio in depth.

Once you create the **Visual Recognition** service instance, you'll create a `Classifier` that you will train with your data.

Creating an instance of Watson Visual Recognition and a classifier

Follow these basic steps to create your service instance:

1. **Login** to IBM Cloud
2. Head over to the **Catalog**
3. Click on **AI** from the menu on the left
4. Select **Visual Recognition**
5. Select the **Lite** plan and click on **Create** to instantiate your service instance

If you don't remember how to instantiate your service instance, refer back to `Chapter 2`, *Can Machines Converse Like Humans?*, where we looked at how to provision your Watson Assistant service.

Once your service has been provisioned, follow these steps to create your classifier:

1. Click on the **Launch tool** button to launch the tooling.
2. Inside the tooling, you'll create a new classifier. For this example, let's create a classifier that can identify dog breeds.
3. You can do so by clicking the **Create Model** button as seen in the following screenshot:

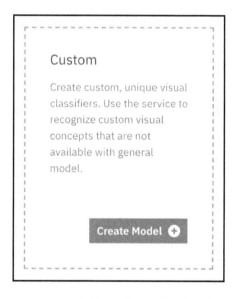

Creating a new Model on Visual Recognition

4. There we go! You should see a new classifier—but it doesn't have a pretty name; let's change that.
5. Click the **pencil** button beside the default classifier name:

Renaming the Visual Recognition Model

6. Give your classifier a name, maybe something such as `Dog Breed Classifier`, and click away from the field.

Uploading data and training the classifier

We need to create some classes that we're interested in, and then load training examples for each of those:

1. Define the classes we'll be using—let's use Golden Retriever, Husky, and Labrador.

2. Click the + icon to add the classes, one at a time. Once you're done, download the data to train the classifier from this book's website: `https://account.packtpub.com/getfile/9781788478298/code`. This data was scraped from Google Images, and it contains nearly 100 images for each class.

3. Unzip the file that you just downloaded, and you will see three nested ZIP files: `husky.zip`, `golden_retriever.zip`, and `labrador.zip`. Drag the ZIP files into the data manager pane on the right in the tooling:

Dragging the ZIPs of images to Watson Studio

4. Associate each ZIP file with the classes you defined a moment ago.

5. You're ready to go! Click the **Train Model** button, and your classifier should start training:

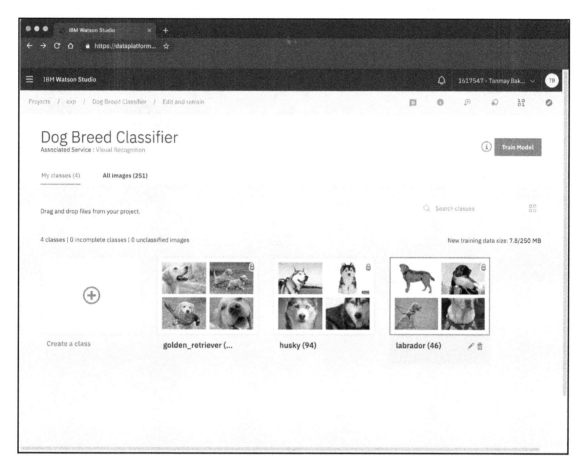

Finding the **Train Model** Button to train your classifier

Testing the classifier

The classifier should take a few minutes to train—but once it's done, you should be able to drag a new image into the tooling, and see the output from Watson. The following screenshot shows Watson being tested on a new image:

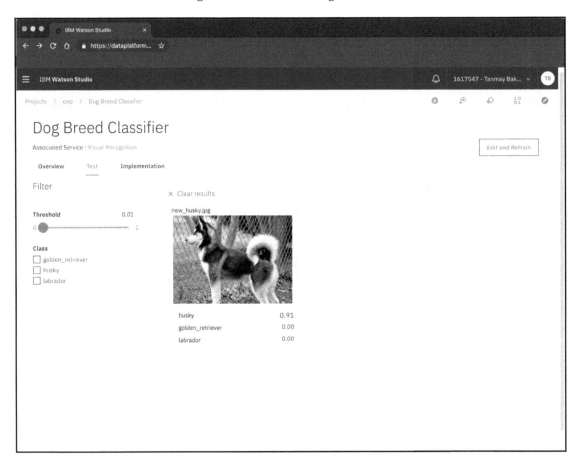

When given an image of a husky that the model wasn't trained on, Watson still successfully classifies the image as a husky.

But now, it's time to take a look at the classifier's functionality in Python.

Creating a Python application to classify with Watson

As mentioned, the application we're building will classify images of dogs based on their breed.

Once the classifier has been trained, we'll create a simple Python application that can take either a URL of an image, or a local image, and run it against the classifier to ascertain the breed.

You'll need two pieces of information to run the classifier in Python: your **API key** and **classifier ID**. The API key will be used to identify your service instance, and the classifier ID is to differentiate between different models within the instance:

1. To get your API key, head over to the **Credentials** tab on your service instance on the IBM Cloud interface, just as you did in Chapter 2, *Can Machines Converse like Humans?*.

2. To get your classifier ID, open the tooling, click on your classifier, and under the classifier name toward the middle, on the **Model ID** row,, you should see your classifier ID:

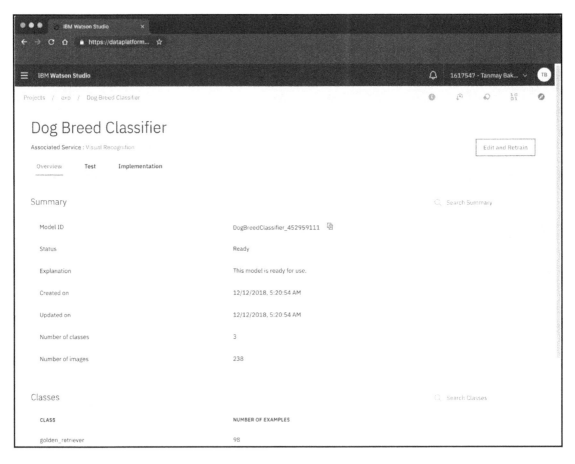

Finding the Classifier ID for your model

Once that's done, you can start coding:

1. Import the `json` library and the service into your script:

```
import json
from ibm_watson.visual_recognition_v3 import VisualRecognitionV3
```

2. Initialize your service instance:

```
visual_recognition =
    VisualRecognitionV3(iam_apikey="<YOUR_API_KEY>")
```

3. Fill in your API key in the `iam_apikey` argument in the preceding code. We are ready to run some inference:

```
classification = visual_recognition.classify(images_file,
        classifier_ids=["DogBreedClassifier_452959111"]
    ).get_result()
```

4. The result is in the form of a JSON string—if you print it out, you should see your result. This is the final code:

[code_1_classify_dogs.py]

```
1.    from ibm_watson.visual_recognition_v3 \
2.        import VisualRecognitionV3
3.
4.    visual_recognition = VisualRecognitionV3(
5.        api_key="unBcJ-zq5gaguq7g6rQnpu9K-1ue8yKvoclgqMf7wMLx",
6.        version="2018-03-19")
7.
8.    with open('./example_goldenretriever.jpg', 'rb') \
9.         as images_file:
10.        classes = visual_recognition.classify(images_file,
11.            classifier_ids=["DogBreedClassifier_452959111"]
12.          ).get_result()
13.        print(json.dumps(classes, indent=2))
```

5. Run it and you should get the following result:

```
{
  "images": [
    {
      "classifiers": [
        {
          "classifier_id": "DogBreedClassifier_452959111",
          "name": "Dog Breed Classifier",
          "classes": [
            {
              "class": "golden_retriever",
              "score": 0.908
            }
          ]
        }
```

```
                    }
                ],
                "image": "example_goldenretriever.jpg"
            }
        ],
        "images_processed": 1,
        "custom_classes": 3
    }
```

If you're wondering what's next, don't: you're done! In under an hour, you are able to upload training data to Watson, train a classifier to recognize dog breeds, and create a Python classifier to access this output.

Handling the case where you don't have training data

As you can see, training machine learning algorithms is a data-intensive task. You need to provide enough data for Watson to understand patterns. However, there are some use cases where you may not have this data. There are two things you can do: gather the data yourself, or use a built-in classifier.

Watson comes with several very accurate built-in classifiers for very common categories. Here are some of the models:

- Facial detection
- Food recognition
- Default (common categories) with color recognition
- Explicit content detection

So, for example, if you were building an application to estimate an Instagram user's age, you could run Watson's facial detection across all of their images, find the most often recurring face using OpenFace—an open source CNN-based facial embedding system—and then you could average the ages that Watson returned for that face.

If you want to build an application to determine the most visually-prominent color in the image (not just the average RGB or highest RGB), you could do that with the default model, since it comes with color recognition.

Let's take a look at a few examples of using built-in models.

Using the facial detection model

Take a look at this photo:

Tanmay and Rob at IBM's Astor Place office

Let's say you wanted to crop out the faces from this image and predict the ages based on the faces. You would use very similar code to what you used for your own classifier—the only difference is that you're going to use the `faces` classifier ID.

This is the code you used last time:

```
[code_1_classify_dogs.py]

1.    from ibm_watson.visual_recognition_v3 \
2.        import VisualRecognitionV3
3.
4.    visual_recognition = VisualRecognitionV3(
```

```
5.        api_key="unBcJ-zq5gaguq7g6rQnpu9K-1ue8yKvoclgqMf7wMLx",
6.        version="2018-03-19")
7.

8.  with open('./example_goldenretriever.jpg', 'rb') \
9.       as images_file:
10.      classes = visual_recognition.classify(images_file,
11.         classifier_ids=["DogBreedClassifier_452959111"]
12.         ).get_result()
13.      print(json.dumps(classes, indent=2))
```

Let's change that to work with the new classifier ID, and then crop out the faces using Pillow, which is an image-manipulation library for Python.

1. Let's create a function that can use Pillow to crop those faces:

   [Chp3-Program-1.py]

   ```
   1 def crop_face(original_image, face_name, watson_face_location):
   2     left = watson_face_location['left']
   3     top = watson_face_location['top']
   4     right = left + watson_face_location['width']
   5     bottom = top + watson_face_location['height']
   6     original_image.crop((left, top, right,
   bottom)).save(face_name)
   ```

2. Let's put it all together with the rest of the code:

   [Chp3-Program-2.py]

   ```
   1.    visual_recognition = VisualRecognitionV3(
   2.       '2018-03-19',
   3.       iam_apikey='unBcJ-zq5gaguq7g6rQnpu9K-1ue8yKvoclgqMf7wMLx')
   4.
   5.  with open('./rob_and_tanmay.jpg', 'rb') as images_file:
   6.      faces = visual_recognition.detect_faces(images_file
   7.              ).get_result()
   8.    for (faceID, face) in \
   9.            enumerate(faces['images'][0]['faces']):
   10.        filename = str(faceID) + "_" + \
   11.           str(face['age']['min']) + '_' + \
   12.           str(face['age']['max']) + \
   13.           face['gender']['gender'] + ".png"
   14.        crop_face(Image.open('./rob_and_tanmay.jpg'),
   15.           filename, face['face_location'])
   ```

This is what your final code should look like:

[code_2_crop_face.py]

```
1.   import json
2.   from ibm_watson.visual_recognition_v3 import
VisualRecognitionV3
3.   from PIL import Image
4.
5.   def crop_face(original_image, face_name, watson_face_location):
6.       left = watson_face_location['left']
7.       top = watson_face_location['top']
8.       right = left + watson_face_location['width']
9.       bottom = top + watson_face_location['height']
10.      original_image.crop((left, top, right, bottom)).\
11.          save(face_name)
12.
13.  visual_recognition = VisualRecognitionV3(
14.      '2018-03-19',
15.      iam_apikey='unBcJ-zq5gaguq7g6rQnpu9K-1ue8yKvoclgqMf7wMLx')
16.
17.  with open('./rob_and_tanmay.jpg', 'rb') as images_file:
18.      faces = visual_recognition.detect_faces(images_file).\
19.          get_result()
20.      for (faceID, face) in \
21.              enumerate(faces['images'][0]['faces']):
22.          filename = str(faceID) + "_" +
23.              str(face['age']['min']) + '_' + \
24.              str(face['age']['max']) + '_' + \
25.              face['gender']['gender'] + ".png"
26.          crop_face(Image.open('./rob_and_tanmay.jpg'),
27.              filename, face['face_location'])
```

3. You should be able to pass the Python script an image; it'll use Watson to detect the faces, and then save the cropped faces to the disk with this format:

```
[face_number]_[age_min_bound]_[age_max_bound]_[gender].png
```

When I feed in this photo:

Tanmay and Rob at IBM's Astor Place office

It returns the following photo:

Let's look at the next photo:

As you can see, Watson was able to detect our faces, and predict our ages and genders. For Rob, it predicted the age as between 54 and 57, and for Tanmay, it predicted the age as between 19 and 21. It's very close! By using more images, you can get more precise results.

With this, you should now be able to create practical applications that use the power of machine learning through Watson to understand visual content! Next, let's find out how you can understand even more complex data, such as natural language, using Watson.

Summary

Computer vision has quickly become one of the most common examples of the power of deep learning. There is a plethora of deep learning examples of visual recognition—many of which have a very basic level of accuracy in recognizing objects and classifying them. Watson also uses deep learning for its Visual Recognition service. However, IBM has honed these algorithms, combining them with different techniques to produce a service that achieves superb accuracy, which can do so for custom recognition models with less training data, and with less compute time than many of the leading services on the market.

In this chapter, we looked at what Watson's Visual Recognition service can do out the box; how to customize it with your own set of classifiers and training data; and how to program it.

In the next chapter, we will examine the speech recognition service.

This Is How Computers Speak   4

If you've been around Siri, Alexa, or any number of other devices, including most modern cars and TVs, you will know that computers can speak and listen. For example, you can use Alexa to order more dog food, ask Siri about the weather outside, or even talk to your car to get navigation guidance to your next appointment. They do this through what we refer to as speech synthesis and speech recognition. IBM has been at the forefront of this technology for decades.

This technology was first introduced by IBM in a product called VoiceType in 1997, and then in a more general product called ViaVoice in 1999 (for more information: `https://en.wikipedia.org/wiki/IBM_ViaVoice`). Later, that same technology was licensed through ScanSoft, which then became Nuance. There is a useful library of information on the science of speech processing available at `https://console.bluemix.net/docs/services/speech-to-text/science.html#science`.

Over the years, IBM has continued to enhance speech technology to leverage deep learning models, and now makes it available through Watson as Text to Speech (`https://console.bluemix.net/catalog/services/text-to-speech`) and Speech to Text services (`https://console.bluemix.net/catalog/services/speech-to-text`). We will discuss these services, including how they work and how to get them to work for you.

In this chapter, we will cover the following topics:

- A computer that talks
- Getting fancier with how to speak
- A fun application of the speech service
- Customizing the speech recognition service

A computer that talks

Let's begin with Text to Speech processing.

The basic process for getting the computer to speak is relatively easy:

- Produce the text of what you want to say
- Send the text to the Text to Speech service to generate a sound file
- Play the sound file through the computer's speaker

Let's walk through this process; we'll start by getting the computer to say something such as, *I'm so glad you're here with me today.*

Throughout this chapter, the sample applications will use the `json` library to facilitate printing out JSON structures. In addition, we use the `TextToSpeechV1` and `SpeechToTextV1` packages from the `ibm_watson` SDK library. You will see these included as import statements at the beginning of the sample programs.

1. Building on what we have learned in Chapter 1, *Background, Transition, and the Future of Computing*, Chapter 2, *Can Machines Converse like Humans?*, and Chapter 3, *Computer Vision*, on how to invoke Watson APIs in Python, the code for creating the sound file can look something like this:

   [Chp4-Program-1.py]

   ```
   1.    from ibm_watson import TextToSpeechV1
   2.
   3.    def textSpeech():
   4.
   5.    # Create session with the Text to Speech service
   6.    text_to_speech = TextToSpeechV1(
   7.        iam_apikey='THPYijj30qodXeAl4UnT4bIDyKSZzmrtnBXWve1tg9kX',
   8.        url='https://stream.watsonplatform.net/text-to-speech/api'
   9.        )
   10.
   11.   # Use Text to Speech to create mp3 file
   12.   with open('glad_to_be_here.mp3', 'wb') as audio_file:
   13.       audio_file.write(
   14.           text_to_speech.synthesize(
   15.                   'I\'m so glad you\'re here with me today.',
   16.                   'audio/mp3',
   17.                   'en-US_MichaelVoice'
   18.               ).get_result().content)
   ```

2. The `TextToSpeechV1` function (on line 6, of the preceding code snippet) simplifies programming to the Watson Text to Speech service. It is contained within the `ibm_watson` SDK package.

3. As with earlier examples, we begin by connecting to the Text to Speech service, using the `iam_apikey` (the service credentials) and the URL for the service, passed into the `TextToSpeechV1()` function, which we do on lines 7, and 8.

4. We create and open an MP3 file in the current directory wherever you are running this application on line 12.

5. Then we invoke the `synthesize()` operation on the opened session on line 14, passing in the text that we want to synthesize on line 15, the audio format that we want to be created on line 16 (audio/mp3, in this case), and the voice that we want to use (en-US_Michael, in this case) on line 17.

6. The resulting MP3 stream is written to the previously opened file on line 13.

There are a number of different audio encodings that you can ask Watson to produce when synthesizing this expression. In this instance, we're producing an MP3 file. Other alternatives include `flac`, `ogg`, `wav`, and `webm`. A complete list of available encodings can be found at: `https://console.bluemix.net/docs/services/text-to-speech/http.html#format`.

When we synthesize the expression in this example, we're instructing the Text to Speech service to use the **Michael** voice. You may recognize this voice as the one that was used in the *Jeopardy!* TV program where Watson competed against Ken Jennings and Brad Rutter, or you may recognize it from many of the IBM Watson commercials that you see on TV.

In fact, there are several different voices that you can use in the synthesized result, including two separate female voices with US accents. A complete list of the available voices can be found at `https://console.bluemix.net/docs/services/text-to-speech/http.html#voices`.

Playing sound through the speaker

Of course, now that you have the resulting sound file, you just need to write some code to play it through the speakers on your device. You can, for example, use the PyAudio library (which you can download from https://pypi.org/project/PyAudio/) with the following code to output your WAV file to the speaker:

[Chp4-Program-2.py]

```
1.   import pyaudio
2.   import wave
3.
4.   # Set the standard Chunk-size constant
5.   CHUNK = 1024
6.
7.   # Open the wave file containing the audio stream you want played
8.   wf = wave.open('glad_to_be_here.wav', 'rb')
9.
10.  # Create an instance of the Audio service
11.  p = pyaudio.PyAudio()
12.
13.  # Open a stream object to the speaker
14.  stream = p.open(format=p.get_format_from_width(wf.getsampwidth()),
15.          channels=wf.getnchannels(),
16.          rate=wf.getframerate(),
17.          output=True)
18.
19.  # Get the first chunk of audio from the wave file
20.  data = wf.readframes(CHUNK)
21.
22.  # Write the first chunk of data to the audio stream, and continue to
23.  # read the next chunk to the speaker audio stream until all of the
24.  # data has been read from the wave file.
25.  while data != '':
26.      stream.write(data)
27.      data = wf.readframes(CHUNK)
28.
29.  # Upon completion, stop and close the audio stream,
30.  # and terminate the Audio service
31.  stream.stop_stream()
32.  stream.close()
33.  p.terminate()
```

 Note that this code sample is using a wave encoding produced by Watson.

Getting fancier with how to speak

The voice that is synthesized by Watson, by default, has fairly interesting inflections. Sometimes, however, you will want even more control over how things are said. Watson provides a way to do this with **Speech Synthesizer Markup Language** (**SSML**).

For example, if you wanted your expression to sound more upbeat, you can surround that text with the `<express-as>` XML markup tags, as follows:

```
<express-as type="GoodNews">I'm so glad you're here with me
today.</express-as>
```

Other expression types include `apology` and `uncertainty`.

In addition to the expressive markup, you can also use the voice transformation markup to make the voice sound softer, as follows:

```
<voice-transformation type="Soft">I'm so glad you're here with me
today.</voice-transformation>
```

Alternatively, you can use voice transformation to make the voice sound younger, as follows:

```
<voice-transformation type="Young">I'm so glad you're here with me
today.</voice-transformation>
```

Additionally, you can also control the degree to which these transformations are applied using the `strength` attribute, as follows:

```
<voice-transformation type="Young" strength="30%">I'm so glad you're here
with me today.</voice-transformation>
```

Finally, if you really want to have greater control over the synthesis, you can use the custom transformation type to control `pitch`, `range`, `glottal_tension`, `breathiness`, `rate`, `timbre`, and `timbre_extent`:

```
<voice-transformation type="Custom" breathiness="x-high">I'm so glad you're
here with me today.</voice-transformation>

<voice-transformation type="Custom" rate="fast">I'm so glad you're here
with me today.</voice-transformation>

<voice-transformation type="Custom" glottal_tension="x-low">I'm so glad
you're here with me today.</voice-transformation>
```

Or, you can even combine effects, as follows:

```
<voice-transformation type="Custom" breathiness="x-high" rate="fast"
glottal_tension="x-low">I'm so glad you're here with me today.</voice-
transformation>
```

 At the time of this writing, the `<express-as>` markup only works with the `en-US_AllisonVoice` voice. In addition to this, the `<voice-transformation>` markup only works with the three `en-US` voices.

A complete list of transformation markups can be found at: `https://console.bluemix.net/docs/services/text-to-speech/SSML-transformation.html#custom-transformations`.

Controlling pronunciation

If your application is going to include words with unusual pronunciations, you can direct Watson on how to handle these words properly. For example, you may be familiar with the different way that *wash* is expressed in the Boston area—sounding more like *warsh*. You can control this pronunciation through the use of the `<phenome>` markup in your text. This markup is a part of the Watson **Symbolic Phonetic Representation (SPR)** system.

Watson supports two different SPR symbol alphabets. The first is proprietary to IBM, and the other is based on the international standard: **International Phonetic Alphabet (IPA)**. You can learn more about the IPA at: `https://en.wikipedia.org/wiki/International_Phonetic_Alphabet`. For now, we will concentrate on the proprietary IBM alphabet.

There are distinct alphabets for different national languages. These are detailed further at: `https://console.bluemix.net/docs/services/text-to-speech/SPRs.html#supportedLanguages`. To demonstrate its use in English, and to achieve the Bostonian pronunciation of *wash*, you can mark up your text as follows:

```
It's time to go <phoneme alphabet="ibm" ph="wa.1rS">wash</phoneme> the car.
```

The `<phoneme>` tag surrounds the word that you want to modify. The `alphabet` attribute tells Watson to use the proprietary IBM alphabet. The alternative is the IPA alphabet. The `ph` attribute describes how to pronounce *wash*. In this case, the `wa` sound is pronounced normally. `.1` tells Watson to treat `rsh` as a syllable and to put primary emphasis on it. The `r` sound is pronounced normally, and `S` tells Watson to express a `sh` sound.

Customizing speech synthesis

It is common that Watson will get used within specialized domains that use a lot of uncommon words. For example, workers in the medical domain use a lot of scientific terms that describe different body parts, diagnoses, and treatments. The standard voice model may not know how to pronounce these terms very well.

You can add pronunciations of those words to your own custom voice model by using the same phoneme mechanism described previously. The difference is that in our prior example, the inline phoneme tag makes a temporary change—just for the duration of processing that one word at that time. But you can also make a lasting change to the voice model so that every time it encounters that word, it will know how to pronounce it.

As an example, the dysautonomia term should be pronounced (in the IBM alphabet) like this:

```
<phoneme alphabet="ibm" ph="dIs.1ato.1nomiH">dysautonomia</phoneme>
```

You can add this pronunciation to your own custom voice model. However, to do so, you have to start by creating your own custom model:

1. You can create a custom model in Watson with the following code:

   [Chp4-Program-3.py]

   ```
   1.   voice_model = text_to_speech.create_voice_model(
   2.         'First Model',
   3.         'en-US',
   4.         'First custom voice model'
   5.      ).get_result()
   6.
   7.   customization_id = voice_model.get("customization_id")
   ```

2. The create_voice_model() function invokes the Watson Text to Speech service to create the model.
3. You can give the model any name that you want. In this case, we're calling it First Model. Additionally, en-US is the language of your custom model, and First custom voice model is the description that you want to associate with the model.

The `customization_id` identity is the unique identity of this model. It is produced by Watson at the same time that you create the model. You can retrieve this identity by using the `get()` function on the `voice_model` object that is returned from the previously invoked `create_voice_model()` function.

4. You can now add words to your model using the `add_words()` function, as follows:

   [Chp4-Program-4.py]

```
1.  text_to_speech.add_words(
2.      customization_id,
3.      [{'word': 'dysautonomia',
4.          'translation': '<phoneme alphabet="ibm"' + \
5.              'ph="dIs.1a.to.1nomiH"></phoneme>'}])
```

5. You can pass in the customization ID that you retrieved previously (this tells Watson what customization you want to work with).

6. And, of course, you can add other words, up to 20,000 of them, that are unique and unusual to your domain.

7. If you modify the code to now include your custom model, it will synthesize the resulting expression with the intended pronunciation:

   [Chp4-Program-5.py]

```
1.  with open('glad_to_be_here.mp3', 'wb') as audio_file:
2.      audio_file.write(
3.          text_to_speech.synthesize(
4.              'Doctor! I believe I have Familial
Dysautonomia',
5.              'audio/mp3',
6.              'en-US_MichaelVoice',
7.              customization_id
8.          ).get_result().content)
```

8. In this case, we are opening an MP3 file and writing the synthesized voice results of the text that now includes the `Dysautonomia` word, but is pronounced as expected.

Using sounds-like customization

As you may have noticed, customizing the synthesizer using phonetic spelling can be tedious, as you really need to know the fundamentals of phonetics and the arcane alphabets that are used to represent them. Fortunately, Watson also offers an alternative and, in general, much easier way of customizing the speech engine—by using sounds-like translations.

For example, if you want Watson to pronounce Imgur correctly, you might customize it to say that it sounds like imager, as demonstrated in the following code block:

[Chp4-Program-6]

```
1.    text_to_speech.add_words(
2.            customization_id,
3.            [{'word': 'Imgur','translation': 'imager'}]
4.        )
```

 Note that by eliminating the <phoneme> tag, Watson will simply take the text provided as a sounds-like phrase for the translated word.

Streaming and timing

The Watson Text to Speech service also offers a streaming interface. This is so that you can start sending the output of the synthesis operation just as it is being produced at the service. This is useful, in part, for improving lag time—you don't have to wait for the service to produce the entire file before playing it to the user. This can be especially important if the amount of text being synthesized is particularly large.

However, the streaming interface can also be important if you want to time various actions with the playing of that speech. For example, let's say that your application is running on a social robot, such as Softbank's Pepper robot, and you want it to provide guidance to people with statements such as *The elevator is over there, past the front desk.* You might want the robot to perform a pointing gesture, timed to coincide with the playing of the word *there*:

1. To place timing markers into your synthesized audio, you can include a `<mark>` tag within your text string:

   ```
   "The elevator is over <mark name="point-left"/> there, past the
   front desk."
   ```

2. The `synthesize()` method will then send a message that specifies the exact time that the mark occurs within the speech audio. The message is a JSON structure that indicates the timing from the beginning of the audio stream at which the `point-left` mark occurs:

Remember, this only works with the streaming interface.

```
{
  "marks": [
    ["point-left", 0.5019387755102041]
  ]
}
```

The `mark` message will be sent separately from the audio message, but always before the audio message is sent.

Unfortunately, at the time of writing, IBM has not provided an SDK for Python to invoke the streaming interface, so we're not going to show that to you here. However, there are SDKs for other languages that do support the streaming interface, such as JavaScript. We encourage you to explore the JavaScript SDK further at `https://cloud.ibm.com/apidocs/text-to-speech?code=java`.

A fun application of the speech service

We've provided a sample `funWithSpeech.py` (https://github.com/PacktPublishing/
Cognitive-Computing-with-IBM-Watson/blob/master/Chapter04/funWithSpeech.py)
application that you can use to have fun with the Watson speech service.

> Before using this sample program, you will have to substitute in your own
> username and password for the service instance that you created earlier.

Let's take a look at what this program is doing:

1. The program can take in three optional command-line arguments—the text string
   that you want to synthesize, the voice in which you want it expressed, and
   the `customization-id` of any custom model that you want to use (assuming
   that you created one previously and have the `customization-id` that was
   created with it).
2. The program begins by parsing and testing the inclusion of any of these three
   arguments on the command line in lines 84 through to 103.
3. It reports on what it will be processing on line 106.
4. Then, it invokes the `textSpeech()` function, passing in the arguments that it
   found, if any, on the command line to do the speech synthesis processing on line
   110.
5. The `textSpeech()` function is defined on line 23.
6. The function will automatically create a `TextToSpeechV1` session object using
   the `initTextSpeech()` function, if one is not passed into the function on line 26.
7. It begins by opening a file that it will use to hold the synthesized audio stream on
   line 34. This is just a temporary file to buffer the handoff between the synthesis
   process and the playing of this stream to a speaker.
8. The Watson `synthesize()` function is called on line 38, passing in the text,
   voice, and custom model parameters.
9. The resulting stream is written to the intermediate file on line 37, and then closed
   on line 46.
10. That same file is reopened in read mode on line 53.
11. A `PyAudio` session object is created on line 56.
12. This session is used to open a stream to the speaker on line 59. The stream is
    conditioned by the frame rate and the number of channels captured in the audio
    file.

13. The first chunk of the audio WAV file is read on line 65.

14. The program then iterates through the audio file writing the audio stream to the speaker, and reading the next chunk from the audio file, one chunk at a time, in lines 70 through to 72.

15. The stream is then closed and the session is terminated in lines 77 through to 79.

You can simply invoke this application by passing in the expression that you want to be synthesized, and the voice that you want it expressed in (this is optional), as follows:

```
python funWithSpeech.py "<express-as type=\"GoodNews\"> I'm so glad you
came to see me today. Let's see if we can find a better way of saving for
your kid's education. </express-as>"
```

Have fun with it!

Talking to the computer

As we've discussed previously, if you are using Watson to speak to your users, you will probably also want to use Watson to listen to what they say. This can be accomplished by using the Watson Speech to Text service.

Using this service is as simple and straightforward as using the Text to Speech service:

1. For example, if you've recorded yourself saying *Transfer $250 from Checking to Savings* in a file called `Transfer request.mp3`, the following code can be used to recognize what you're saying and translate it to text:

[Chp4-Program-7.py]

```
1.   import json
2.   from ibm_watson import SpeechToTextV1
3.
4.   # Create a connection to the speech to text service
5.   speech_to_text = SpeechToTextV1(
6.       iam_apikey='f6nEkrdAJdvluiBI74xhnlQ134HcHFxxrL21Krii_0Gg',
7.       url='https://stream.watsonplatform.net/speech-to-text/api')
8.
9.   # Identify the source audio file
10.  file = 'Transfer request.mp3'
11.
12.  # Open the file in the local folder
13.  with open(join(dirname(__file__), './.', file), 'rb') \
14.      as audio_file:
15.
```

```
16.    # Invoke the recognize() function on the speech service
17.    speech_recognition_results = speech_to_text.recognize(
18.       audio=audio_file,                 # File with the audio
19.       content_type='audio/mp3',         # The codec for the file
20.       timestamps=True,                  # Return timing markers?
21.       word_alternatives_threshold=0.9,  # The min interpretation
22.                                         # confidence
23.    ).get_result()
24.
25. # Print out the resulting JSON produced from the translation
26. print(json.dumps(speech_recognition_results, indent=2))
```

2. We begin by creating a connection to the Speech to Text service on line 5.

As usual, you will want to fill in the `username` and `password` variables with those that you got when you created the service on the IBM Cloud.

3. In this example, we assume that you've recorded your voice in an MP3 file (as indicated by its file extension) and have declared so on line 10.

4. We open that file on line 13.

5. Then, we pass it into the `recognize()` function of the speech service on line 17.

6. We declare that the file is encoded as an MP3 file on line 19.

7. We indicate that we want timing marks included in the resulting translation.

8. `word_alternative_threshold` is essentially indicating the level of confidence that we want Watson to have when interpreting a given word before starting to look for alternative words in the context of the previously translated sentence fragment.

Getting voice from a microphone

Typically, you will want to create your file by inputting directly from the microphone. Again, we can leverage any number of available Python libraries for this.

We demonstrate how to do this using the `PyAudio` library in the following code example:

[Chp4-Program-8.py]

```
1.    import pyaudio
2.    import wave
3.
4.    # Set the constants that will be used in this program
```

```
5.    FORMAT = pyaudio.paInt16      # The word size to get from the microphone
6.    CHANNELS = 2                  # Read the microphone in stereo
7.    RATE = 44100                  # Read the microphone at 44Khz
8.    CHUNK = 1024                  # Encode the audio in 1KB chunks
9.    RECORD_SECONDS = 5            # Record for a maximum of 5 seconds
10.
11.   # Put the recorded sound in this file
12.   WAVE_OUTPUT_FILENAME = "speechInput.wav"
13.
14.   #
15.   # The getAudio() function will capture audio from the microphone and
16.   # record in the file specified above.
17.   def getAudio():
18.
19.       # Create a PyAudio session object
20.       audio = pyaudio.PyAudio()
21.
22.       # Open the microphone for recording
23.       stream = audio.open(format=FORMAT, channels=CHANNELS,
24.               rate=RATE, input=True,
25.               frames_per_buffer=CHUNK)
26.
27.       # Indicate to the user they can start talking
28.       print("recording...")
29.
30.       # Create a vector in which to append chunks of audio
31.       frames = []
32.
33.       # Continue to read from the microphone and append chunks of audio
34.       # to the frames vector
35.       for i in range(0, int(RATE / CHUNK * RECORD_SECONDS)):
36.           data = stream.read(CHUNK)
37.           frames.append(data)
38.
39.       # Tell the user the microphone is being turned off
40.       print("finished recording")
41.
42.       # Stop the reecording and close the input stream
43.       stream.stop_stream()
44.       stream.close()
45.       audio.terminate()
46.
47.       # Now write the audio frames vector out to a Wave file
48.       waveFile = wave.open(WAVE_OUTPUT_FILENAME, 'wb')
49.       waveFile.setnchannels(CHANNELS)
50.       waveFile.setsampwidth(audio.get_sample_size(FORMAT))
51.       waveFile.setframerate(RATE)
52.       waveFile.writeframes(b''.join(frames))
```

```
53.        waveFile.close()
54.
55.        # And return the resulting file
56.        return WAVE_OUTPUT_FILENAME
57.
58.   #
59.   # This is the main body of the program that prompts the user to say
60.   # something, and then invokes the getAudio() function to record them
61.   # from the microphone.
62.   #
63.   print("Say what you want.")
64.   audioFileName = getAudio()
```

Recognizing more than one speaker: This particular example will record your voice for 5 seconds. Under more realistic circumstances, you will want to test each chunk of sound for whether they contain any discernable sound, and after a short period, you can assume the user has stopped speaking.

1. This program contains the getAudio() function, as defined on line 17.
2. The getAudio() function begins by creating a PyAudio session object on line 20.
3. It then opens a microphone stream on line 23, parameterized by the constants that were created earlier in lines 5 through to 8.
4. It notifies the user that the recording has started on line 28.
5. The frames object created on line 31 is a vector that will be used to collect the audio received from the microphone as a vector of audio chunks.
6. It then enters into a loop for 5 seconds (as set in the RECORD_SECONDS constant on line 9) in which it reads a chunk of audio from the microphone and appends that to the frames vector in lines 35 through to 37.
7. The program lets the user know that recording has stopped on line 40.
8. Then, it closes the audio stream and terminates the PyAudio session in lines 43 through to 45.
9. The audio is then written to the output file, along with channel, sample width, and frame rate metadata in lines 48 through to 53, with the file being returned from the function on line 56.
10. The main body of the program begins on line 63 with the user being prompted to say something, followed by calling the getAudio() function on line 64.

Using the WebSockets interface to speech recognition

If you want more control over the speech recognition interaction, you can use the WebSockets interface for the Speech to Text service. One of the great benefits of the WebSockets interface is that it will give you interim results as the speech service is evaluating what is said. Besides giving you fascinating insights into how the speech engine works, its real-time feedback can be useful for helping users refine their own enunciation to help the engine do a better job of understanding the user.

Moreover, when you combine the WebSockets-based interface for speech recognition with streaming directly from a microphone on your machine, you can create a very speedy and responsive application for real-time speech recognition. To know more, you can refer to the following link: https://console.bluemix.net/docs/services/speech-to-text/websockets.html#websockets.

We've created a similar application in Python in the microphoneSpeech.py sample program. This sample makes use of two helper programs: StreamSpeechService.py and TextSpeechService.py.

Let's begin by explaining the TextSpeechService.py (https://github.com/PacktPublishing/Cognitive-Computing-with-IBM-Watson/blob/master/Chapter04/TextSpeechService.py) program:

1. The TextSpeechService.py program provides a pair of helper classes for Text to Speech processing. The initTextSpeech() function on line 8 simply creates a connection to the Watson text-to-speech service. Remember to update this with your API credentials for your service instance.

2. The textSpeech() function on line 14 will convert a text string that you provide into a synthesized voice, using the Text to Speech service session that you created with initTextSpeech(). It does so by putting the resulting synthesized sound into a WAV file, called glad_to_be_here.wav, in your current directory, and then piping that file to your speakers using the PyAudio library.

Now let's discuss the StreamSpeechService.py (https://github.com/ PacktPublishing/Cognitive-Computing-with-IBM-Watson/blob/master/Chapter04/ StreamSpeechService.py) helper program:

1. The SpeechStreamService.py program also provides a set of helper classes for speech-to-text processing. The initSpeechText() function on line 23 will create a connection to the Watson Speech to Text service. As before, make sure that you substitute in your own API credentials for your service instance, but also be sure to avoid confusing this with the Text to Speech service.

2. The recognizeUsingWebSocket() function on line 32 is the main routine initiating the recognition operation on the speech service. It is contained within a Python function, because this function will be placed on its own thread of execution (we'll talk about this later when we examine the main program).

3. The pyaudio_callback() function on line 48 is how PyAudio updates the program with any block of sound that it picks up from the microphone. The callback is invoked one CHUNK at a time (note that the CHUNK size is a constant that is set when the PyAudio session, is established). The function makes use of a QUEUE stream that is created outside of the function but passed in through a variable that is global to the entire module.

4. The StreamSpeechControl class defined on line 59 is the central point of communication between the main thread, the speech thread, and its callback service. The QUEUE stream used by pyaudio_callback(), along with an instance of the PyAudio session are both created in the constructor of the StreamSpeechControl object on lines 70 and 71.

5. An instance of an AudioSource object will be needed by the Speech to Text service to supply the audio stream. This object is also created within the constructor for the StreamSpeechControl object on line 72 and initialized with the same QUEUE stream that was supplied to PyAudio as a callback. It is through this connection that the microphone audio is piped into the Speech to Text transcription service. In addition, we create an instance of the MyRecognizeCallback object on line 73, and initialize a session to the Speech to Text service by invoking initSpeechText() function on line 74.

6. The createQueue() method on line 77 simply creates the QUEUE stream, initialized with a buffer space that is 10 times the size of the CHUNK constant. Note that this is an estimate of the maximum space that is needed to buffer the microphone audio to the Speech to Text service. If this buffer gets full, audio packets will be discarded, which will affect the accuracy of speech recognition. So, if you suspect that this is happening, you may want to increase the buffer size.

7. The `endQueue()` method on line 83 will just flush the `QUEUE` stream. This is used between the periods of using the microphone to keep older audio from interfering with new speech.

8. The `initAudio()` method on line 87 opens the `PyAudio` connection with the microphone, setting the `pyaudio_callback()` function for buffering the microphone audio.

9. The `terminateAudio()` method on line 99 is the corollary of the `initAudio()` method—closing the microphone stream.

10. The `MyRecognizeCallback` class on line 105 is part of the Speech to Text system and is used by the `recognize_use_websocket()` service to report on its progress. This inherits from the `RecognizeCallback` class provided by the Python SDK for the Watson speech recognition service. The methods in this class override the base methods and can be used to process the results of its progress.

11. The `constructor()` method on line 112 must be implemented to initiate the constructor of the parent class.

12. The `on_hypothesis()` method on line 119 is called by Watson to report any intermediate interpretations the service concludes from what it is hearing. We've implemented this method to display these intermediate interpretations on the Terminal window to reflect Watson's evolving assessment of what is being said. When watching this in action, you will notice that Watson occasionally goes back and reinterprets what it thinks you likely said, based on what you said next—this is remarkably similar to what we do as humans as we hear more, and that additional context clarifies earlier interpretations of the things that we heard.

13. The `on_transcription()` method on line 128 is called by Watson when it believes that we've concluded speaking and it has a full interpretation of what we have said. This generally occurs when Watson hears us pause or take a breath, or when it has concluded that we've spoken a full phrase or sentence. In this implementation of the method, we report on what Watson concluded, but then also set a flag to indicate to the main thread that Watson has finished interpreting the speech and to start acting on it. We'll discuss this further when we explain the main program logic.

14. The `isTextTranscribed()` method on line 158 is used by the main program logic to test whether a full transcription has been completed.

15. The `getTranscription()` method on line 161 is used by the main program logic to get the text that was transcribed and to optionally reset the flag that was used to indicate that completion. With the text retrieved on the main thread and the flag reset, Watson is free to continue listening and evaluating further speech expressions from the microphone stream.

16. Finally, the `setWindow()` method on line 168 is simply used to communicate about the terminal window in which this program will present its progress.

Now, let's spend some time walking through what the main `microphoneSpeech.py` (`https://github.com/PacktPublishing/Cognitive-Computing-with-IBM-Watson/blob/master/Chapter04/microphoneSpeech.py`) program is doing:

1. We will begin by importing the Python `Curses` package that comes in Python to provide a more controlled user output experience, and so we import that on line 1.

2. We will be using multithreading in this program, and so we have imported the threads library on line 2.

3. As usual, we have to begin by importing all of the services that we will be using from the Watson SDK, which we do on lines 4 and 5.

4. The `helper` functions that we described previously are imported on lines 6 and 7.

5. This program starts out by creating a connection to the Text to Speech service on line 17, which it will use later to also report on the interpretation of your speech, and sets the default voice to use in this program on line 18.

6. This program, on line 21, then creates an instance of `StreamSpeechControl`. As we described earlier, the constructor for the `StreamSpeechControl` object also creates a `QUEUE` object, which it sets in a global variable, and an instance of `PyAudio` and `AudioSource` objects, which are set in instance variables of the object.

7. The program then goes on to spawn a separate thread on lines 24 and 25 to process the `recognizeUsingWebsocket()` function, and passes in the `SPEECH_CONTROL` object created previously.

8. Now, both the main thread and the speech processing thread have access to the control object and its shared information. In the process of initiating the separate thread, the `recognizeUsingWebsocket()` function will create an instance of the `MyRecognizeCallback` class, which is also set in the `SPEECH_CONTROL` object, and then initiates the `recognize_using_websocket()` service, passing in the callback object that it just created, and the `AudioSource` object that was created earlier during the construction of the `SPEECH_CONTROL` object.

9. Next, on line 29, the program will create a terminal window that it will use to report progress to the user and set a reference to that window in the `SPEECH_CONTROL` object on line 30.

10. Next, the program goes into a loop on line 34 that will continue until the user quits the program.

11. In this loop, we erase the terminal window and prompt the user to say something on lines 36 to 39.

12. This code is also written to work even if you modify it to avoid creating a `termWindow` object with the additional logic captured on lines 40 and 41.

13. On line 44, we open the microphone and wait on line 47 for the user to say something and the speech service to interpret what was said. The processing of this speech interpretation is actually occurring on the other thread that we spawned previously, so we just have to wait until the service has concluded its interpretation of the user's speech. The test on line 47 will indicate when that interpretation has been completed.

14. At this point we get the transcribed text on line 51, which also resets the callback for the next time we use it, and close the microphone on line 54 so that we avoid picking up any other background noise.

15. The transcribed results will contain several pieces of information, including the level of confidence that the service has in its interpretation and the text that it received from this interpretation, which is parsed from the transcription on lines 57 and 58.

16. We test for whether the user wanted to quit the program on line 61, and if so we break out of the loop to end the program on line 62.

17. At this point, we can go on to process the utterance offered by the user. Here, we formulate different responses based on the level of confidence Watson has in its interpretation on lines 64 through 72. On line 75, we vocalize this response to the user through the Text to Speech service using the helper method that we defined in the `TextSpeechService` module.

18. If the user did express their intent to quit the program, we terminate the loop and go on to close the terminal window on line 78, say our goodbyes, and terminate the audio and `Audio_Source` streams on lines 80 and 81.

19. There is no way of killing a thread in Python, so we just let it terminate along with the program.

When you run the `microphoneSpeech.py` (https://github.com/PacktPublishing/Cognitive-Computing-with-IBM-Watson/blob/master/Chapter04/microphoneSpeech.py) program, you should get a terminal window that will look something like the following screenshot after you've said *I'd like to transfer $20 from checking to savings*:

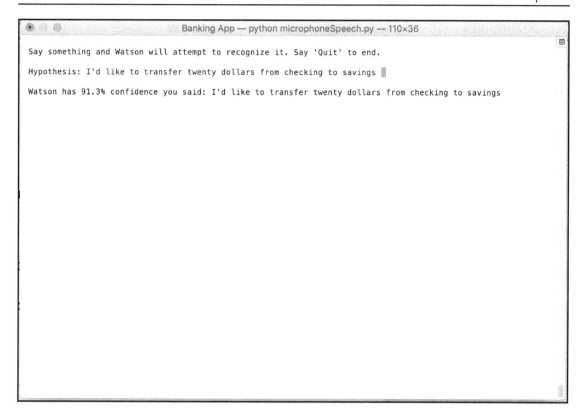

```
Banking App — python microphoneSpeech.py — 110×36

Say something and Watson will attempt to recognize it. Say 'Quit' to end.

Hypothesis: I'd like to transfer twenty dollars from checking to savings

Watson has 91.3% confidence you said: I'd like to transfer twenty dollars from checking to savings
```

You may encounter a few occasions where you want Watson to listen to multiple users at the same time. For example, you may introduce a conversational agent into a meeting that you're holding and need Watson to transcribe the discussion between different participants in the meeting. Alternatively, you may want to transcribe the conversation between a client and an agent during a call-center session.

It turns out Watson can recognize the vocal differences of up to six different speakers, although it works best with fewer users:

1. To activate Watson's ability to distinguish between voices, you must set the speaker_labels argument on the recognize() service to true, like this:

```
speech_service.recognize_using_websocket(
        audio=speechControl.AUDIO_SOURCE,
        content_type='audio/l16; rate=44100',
        recognize_callback=speechControl.MYCALLBACK,
        interim_results=True,
        speaker_labels=True
    )
```

2. Having done so, Watson will now begin to report its observations about the different speakers in the response data. This information shows up in a JSON structure—either in its return from the `recognize()` service, or in the `on_data()` method of the `RecognizeCallback` class (the `MyRecognizeCallback` concrete class from our preceding example) if you use the `recognize_using_websocket()` service. The reported JSON might look as follows:

[Chp4-JSON-1.json]

```
1     {
2        "speaker_labels": [
3           {
4              "to": 11.67,
5              "confidence": 0.382,
6              "speaker": 2,
7              "from": 11.44,
8              "final": false
9           },
10          {
11             "to": 11.8,
12             "confidence": 0.382,
13             "speaker": 2,
14             "from": 11.67,
15             "final": false
16          },
17          {
18             "to": 11.89,
19             "confidence": 0.382,
20             "speaker": 2,
21             "from": 11.8,
22             "final": false
23          },
24          {
25             "to": 12.41,
26             "confidence": 0.382,
27             "speaker": 2,
28             "from": 11.89,
29             "final": false
30          },
31          {
32             "to": 16.07,
33             "confidence": 0.446,
34             "speaker": 0,
35             "from": 15.81,
36             "final": false
37          },
```

```
38        {
39              "to": 39.55,
40              "confidence": 0.48,
41              "speaker": 2,
42              "from": 38.92,
43              "final": false
44        }
45     ]
46  }
```

Each component of the preceding JSON structure (for example, from lines 3 to 9) reports the timestamps of the beginning and end of the audio segment where this voice was detected, and the level of confidence Watson has in this being the correct voice that it heard. The final element is merely indicating whether the audio recognition stream that Watson is listening to has completed. In this case, the stream is still flowing and, therefore, Watson is not done processing. It's also important to realize that the longer that Watson listens to the various speakers in the stream the better and more confident it will get at distinguishing each speaker.

Also, note that Watson is not actually identifying the speaker. This is not voice identification; it is only distinguishing between speakers in the conversation, and only identifies them as speaker 0, 1, and so on. These identities are sequenced by the order in which that person spoke within the conversation stream. Moreover, considering that Watson's accuracy and confidence are lower earlier in the conversation—specifically at the beginning of the discussion—Watson may even swap its understanding of which speaker is which as the conversation goes on.

Telephones are not good microphones

In the late 19th and early 20th century, when the telephone system infrastructure was being built, one of the issues that engineers faced with was how to deal with the relatively poor quality of telephone equipment. Later, it became the issue of how to multiplex many concurrent conversations over limited networking resources. To handle these problems, the decision was made to limit the frequency over which voice would be transmitted to between 300 Hz and 3,400 Hz. This frequency range is sufficient for people to understand each other. However, this is a relatively narrow range compared to what the human ear can naturally hear, and so it is referred to as narrowband communication. This frequency band has remained as the standard for most telephony recordings. And, as you can imagine, listening to and recognizing speech over the narrowband requires special training. This is different from what is needed to hear and understand speech over the full spectrum that humans can hear—otherwise referred to as broadband.

Watson supports both narrowband and broadband speech recognition. You should select the band that is appropriate for your application. If you are connected to the telephony network, use narrowband. If you're pulling your audio stream from a live microphone, then you will be better off using the broadband model.

To select which you want to use, specify your model preference on the `model` parameter of the `recognize()` service.

This also takes us to the discussion of base models.

More about base models

People from different countries have different accents, and they generally speak different languages or dialects. Sometimes, these differences even exist in different regions of the same country. If you've ever been to a place where people speak differently, perhaps with a different dialect or with a different accent, then you may find it hard to understand what they're saying at first. You have to train your ear to understand how they say and pronounce things.

The same is true for Watson.

To assist this, IBM has created a set of models that have been trained for how people commonly speak in different countries, factoring in their language and accents. These are known as base models. For the examples in *Talking to the computer* and *Using the WebSockets interface to speech recognition* section, we have been using the `en-US_BroadbandModel` model, which is the default model for the speech system. `en` is for English, and `US` is for the accent and dialect of English that is commonly used in the US.

 Note that the model is also conditioned as being a broadband versus narrowband model—you express the language, locale, and bandwidth when identifying which base model that you want to use.

Watson has models for some 18 different languages, locales, and bandwidth combinations (note that narrowband is not available for all language and locale combinations). A complete list is provided at: `https://console.bluemix.net/docs/services/speech-to-text/input.html#models`.

You can control which base model you want to use in your application with the `model` parameter of the `recognize()` service, as follows:

```
speech_service.recognize_using_websocket(
        audio=speechControl.AUDIO_SOURCE,
        content_type='audio/l16; rate=44100',
        recognize_callback=speechControl.MYCALLBACK,
        interim_results=True,
        model='en-US_BroadbandModel'
    )
```

In places where your audience may be multicultural and multilingual, you can't instruct Watson to listen with a multiple number of different models on the same connection, but you can set up multiple service calls and pipe the same audio to each of those instances in parallel to see which one does a better job of recognizing the user. Just bear in mind that you will be charged for each additional service call you make—essentially multiplying the cost of using the service. But, this may be an appropriate thing to do in some scenarios.

Finally, you should also note that not all base models support speaker labeling; these restrictions are listed at `https://console.bluemix.net/docs/services/speech-to-text/output.html#speaker_labels`.

Dealing with speaker hesitations

We often hesitate while we're talking—usually, it is because we're trying to think about what we want to say, or because we are remembering things that are key to what we're trying to do, and also because, sometimes, we just get distracted.

Watson handles this in a couple of ways, depending on how long the speaker hesitates for. If the hesitation is short or done using a filler word, such as *umm*, Watson will add this into its interpretation with the **%HESITATION** word. Actually, Watson uses different filler words for different languages. For these cases, it's normal to just look for those words and filter them out of your text stream.

In other cases, where the hesitation is long—that is, longer than the timeout interval—Watson will assume that you have finished speaking and finalize its interpretation of what you said. You can handle this is a couple of ways. If it happens a lot, you can increase the `inactivity_timeout` parameter to the `recognize()` service, as follows:

```
speech_service.recognize_using_websocket(
        audio=speechControl.AUDIO_SOURCE,
        content_type='audio/l16; rate=44100',
        recognize_callback=speechControl.MYCALLBACK,
        interim_results=True,
        inactivity_timeout=45
    )
```

In this case, we have set it to 45 seconds, but you may want to experiment to determine the optimal value for your application.

If your application uses a natural language classifier, such as the Watson Assistant service, and if that service responds to an utterance interpreted by the speech service indicating that it couldn't classify it, or at least without a high level of confidence, then you can try appending the utterance with whatever follows to see if that combined utterance is more recognizable, and perhaps indicative of the user having paused between major fragments of their speech.

Customizing the speech recognition service

As is the case with virtually all Watson services, you can customize your instance of Watson speech. In this case, the Speech to Text service has two models that can be customized—a language model and an acoustic model—both of which will be explained further.

Customizing Watson's language model

The language model tells Watson about new words to listen out for. In essence, the custom language models expand Watson's vocabulary. You will not provide any acoustic signature for these vocabulary words, rather you simply create an entry for these words, their display spelling, and its various (one or more) sounds-like phonetic spellings (refer to the *Using sounds-like customization* section of this chapter).

Watson provides two different ways of adding to its vocabulary. The easier approach is to provide a text document that exemplifies the type of vocabulary that is used in your domain. Watson will parse this document and add any words it does not already know about. While easier, this approach gives you less control over sounds-like mappings.

The other approach is to add each word (or set of words) through individual calls to Watson.

Customizing the language model is more advanced than we want to get into in this book, but IBM does provide a useful sample Python script for using this customization at `https:/ /console.bluemix.net/docs/services/speech-to-text/language-create. html#exampleScripts`.

Note that this example does not use the Python SDK for Speech to Text so it is showing you the raw HTTP request processing of the service. You will want to pay special attention to how these same operations are performed with the SDK by reading the API Reference at `https://www. ibm.com/watson/developercloud/speech-to-text/api/v1/python.html? python#create-language-model`.

If you remember back to when we customized the Text to Speech service earlier in this chapter, we had to first create a custom model, from which we got back `customization_id`. The same thing holds true here as well. You will create a custom model using the `create_language_model()` service. In doing so, you must specify which base model you intend to customize, and give it a name and description that is relevant to your application.

You will later use `customization_id` when you invoke the `recognize` service, as follows:

```
speech_service.recognize_using_websocket(
    audio=speechControl.AUDIO_SOURCE,
    content_type='audio/l16; rate=44100',
    recognize_callback=speechControl.MYCALLBACK,
    interim_results=True,
    customization_id="ce92f3e8-0e76-4b87-b768-21c38e078bcb",
    customization_weight=0.7
)
```

You will have to update the ID with the string that you got back from Watson when you created the custom model.

In addition to specifying a custom language model, you can also specify the weight that should be applied to this additional vocabulary when evaluating the speech of the user with the use of the `customization_weight` parameter. The amount of influence this additional vocabulary has on overall speech processing is highly conditional on how dominant these words are within the speech of the users. You will have to experiment with this value to find a weight that is optimal for your circumstances.

Customizing the acoustic model for Watson

The other thing that you can customize is Watson's acoustic model. You will want to do this when the environment in which the user is speaking is unusually loud, or where the microphone setup is different, or where the user speaks with an unusually heavy accent (for example, not speaking in their native language). In any of these cases, you can train Watson to hear through these background noises, acoustic aberrations, or accents.

To train Watson on these acoustic differences, you need to supply Watson with a sample of people talking within these acoustic conditions.

Start by collecting recordings of that situation. You can record this in multiple separate files, but you must have at least 10 minutes of recording (in which people are actually speaking), but no more than 50 hours in total. No one file (or any one archive of files) can be more than 100 MB in size. The files can be recorded in any of the supported audio types (`wav`, `mp3`, and more; you can refer to `https://console.bluemix.net/docs/services/speech-to-text/audio-formats.html#audio-formats`), but must be at a sampling rate (narrowband or broadband) that matches the base model with which you will be using the custom model.

You can then create an acoustic model, and then add these recordings to that model—either one file at a time or a set of files in an archive (`.zip` or `.tar.gz`).

While this is optional, it is even better if you combine the acoustic model with a custom language model that corresponds to the things being said in the acoustic model. Ideally, the language model will contain a verbatim transcript of the conversation presented within the acoustic model—something that was perhaps typed up by someone transcribing the audio recording. Watson will then leverage that language model to improve its recognition accuracy.

As with the language model, the acoustic model that you create will be assigned an identity string that you can specify when invoking the recognition service. The language model and the acoustic model will be assigned distinct IDs. You will use the `acoustic_customization_id` parameter to specify your acoustic model when invoking the `recognize` service, as follows:

```
speech_service.recognize_using_websocket(audio=speechControl.AUDIO_SOURCE,
        content_type='audio/l16; rate=44100',
        recognize_callback=speechControl.MYCALLBACK,
        interim_results=True,
        customization_id="ce92f3e8-0e76-4b87-b768-21c38e078bcb",
        customization_weight=0.7,
        acoustic_customization_id= \
            "fd184a79-2b22-41e2-8d7d-324cdc79247e",
    )
```

For both custom language models and custom acoustic models, you cannot use these models until you've trained them. Training is performed as a distinct step using the `train_language_model()` and `train_acoustic_model()` services, respectively. Both of these services simply initiate the training process as a background job (executing in the cloud). It can take anywhere from a couple of minutes to several hours to complete training—depending on the size of the training data and the load on the system.

Once you've kicked off a training cycle, you can monitor its progress using the `get_language_model()` or `get_acoustic_model()` services.

Leveraging batch processing

Sometimes, you will have a collection of audio recordings that you want transcribing. For example, perhaps you run a call center where all of your calls are recorded, and now you want those transcribed so that you can do text processing on them. You can batch process these recordings using Watson's Speech to Text asynchronous `create_job()` service.

You can optionally supply a callback service that will be invoked by Watson to provide status updates on the progress of the job. To do this, you must first create and register a callback service with an addressable URL (something that Watson will be able to reach through your firewall) using the `register_callback()` service. The registration process tests whether the callback service is addressable and authentic.

Once the registration process has been performed (and validated), you can go on to submit a job, passing in the file that you want transcribing, and identifying the URL for the callback service.

If you don't supply a callback service when you create the job, you can simply poll the asynchronous job service for progress using the `check_job()` or `check_jobs()` services depending on whether you have one or multiple jobs in flight.

Summary

Interacting with your computer (or computer-driven device) through natural vocalized speech adds a whole new dimension to human-machine interfaces. On the one hand, it adds both convenience and efficiency, avoiding the need to type everything in through a keyboard. In many cases, a voice interface can open up a whole range of uses that previously had been locked out. If you're driving a car or operating heavy machinery, you need both hands to operate them safely—it's just never a good idea to be staring at a keyboard while you type when traveling at 60 miles an hour.

On the other hand, talking to your computer can also take some getting used to. For many of us, it is socially awkward to be talking to your toaster in the middle of a dinner party, or to be dictating out loud your medical problems to your phone on an elevator full of strangers. This may get easier as social norms shift, but some of these scenarios will likely always need other forms of input to help protect our privacy in public settings.

Nonetheless, voice interfaces are already surfacing in many of the products that we use today, and this trend will only increase over time. Moreover, the use of voice interfaces is the first major step towards forms of AI embodiments that will enable AI-based computers and devices to create a stronger sense of presence within our daily routines.

In this chapter, we've shown you how you can synthesize a voice for the computer to talk to your users, and how to use a microphone (or other recording devices) to understand their vocal input. We've gone on to explain how to customize either of these in particular scenarios.

In the next chapter, we will explain how Watson recognizes human empathy.

Further reading

If you would like to find out more about what we talked in this chapter, here are some more resources:

- The original *Jeopardy!* game show in which Watson competed against Ken Jennings and Brad Rutter can be seen here: https://www.youtube.com/watch?v=P18EdAKuC1U.
- You can find out more about Softbank's Pepper Robot here: https://www.softbankrobotics.com/emea/en/pepper.

5
Expecting Empathy from Dumb Computers

For millions of years, empathy has evolved in human beings, and has played a big part in increasing the complexity and strength of social interactions at the person-to-person level. What if we could take this just a fraction of this ability of ours, and allow computers to understand empathy as well? That's what we'll talk about in this chapter.

In this chapter, we're going to cover the following topics:

- Introducing empathy
- Understanding the complexities of sentiment
- The functionality of the Tone Analyzer API
- Using natural language to predict personality traits
- Calling the Personality Insights API

Introducing empathy

Empathy is complex. Many animals show signs of understanding the concept of empathy; of course, humans do, as do chimps, elephants, and crows.

To get an understanding of how complex it truly is, and how simple we think it is, if I were to ask you when you learned empathy, what would you answer? You'd probably think it's a trick question. But you'd be wrong—empathy is a learned skill; it's acquired, just like human facial recognition.

The Oxford Dictionary defines empathy as the ability to understand and share the feelings of another.

In this chapter, while we won't simulate the ability to understand feelings per se, we will create an application that can understand the intended sentiment of a certain natural language passage.

From there, we'll take a look at another aspect of empathy—understanding an individual's personality based on the way they write.

Understanding the complexities of sentiment

Sentiment is complex because it's a human feeling, and it's represented in an unstructured, human way; that is, natural language. Natural language is one of the most complex kinds of unstructured data—if not the most complex. There's a lot of ambiguity, and you need to understand the context of everything for anything to make sense.

If, for example, Stephanie were to say this in a conversation—*I shot an elephant in my pyjamas.*

If you had no idea what was said before or after this, how would you understand this sentence?

Well, you may say that the sentence means that Stephanie took a picture of an elephant while Stephanie was in her pyjamas. You'd technically be right, but the same sentence could mean that Stephanie was hunting the elephant, maybe while the elephant was wearing Stephanie's pyjamas.

Both of those interpretations have wildly different meanings, and probably evoke very different sentiments, depending on how you feel about photographing versus hunting elephants that may or may not be dressed in horribly-fitting bed clothes.

If, however, you had some more context, such as the fact that Stephanie works as a photographer, then you could make a more informed decision or interpretation. You could say that Stephanie is a human, humans are animals, elephants are also animals, but humans are the only animals associated with clothing, and pyjamas are a kind of clothing, and Stephanie works as a photographer, and photographers take pictures, and shot as a verb may mean the action of taking a picture!

This run-on sentence was the reasoning that would go behind understanding that single small sentence about elephants. Watson doesn't do all of this reasoning through the Tone Analyzer API. However, Watson does use machine learning to discern patterns in the way humans use certain tones in natural language.

Watson's not just doing keyword matching, it's not just assigning a sentiment score to each word—it's understanding that word in context with all the other words in order to give you an analysis.

In fact, the Tone Analyzer can also understand sentiment in conversations, which is something that we'll talk about toward the end of this section. Before that, let's start with a quick walk through on how to use the Tone Analyzer.

One thing you should note: the two services that you're going to use in this chapter—the Tone Analyzer service and the Personality Insights service—don't need to be trained. In fact, they can't be trained, so you will be using the pre-trained models from IBM. You will only be providing your own data for inference.

The functionality of the Tone Analyzer API

With the Tone Analyzer API, as the name implies, you can analyze the tone of a passage of text. These are the six possible tones as shown in the following table:

Tone	Example
Anger	Seriously? I just bought my phone yesterday and it's already bricked!
Fear	I'm worried my phone is going to overheat!
Joy	`#ThisBrand` makes the best chocolate bars!
Sadness	It's too bad that Ken and Brad lost to a computer on Jeopardy!
Analytical	Your computational thinking skills are excellent; however, you need to work on your programming.
Tentative	I'm beginning to wonder if `#ThisPhone` is the best in the market anymore.

When you pass Watson some text, it generates a score for each of these tones on a scale of 0 to 1. It also lets you know which parts of the text activated those scores. So, for example, *The Spongebob Squarepants Out Of Water movie is excellent, I loved it! I do think that the part toward the end could be a bit longer, though.*

The Tone Analyzer returns the following tones, ranked in descending order:

1. Tentative (83%)
2. Joy (78%)
3. Analytical (52%)

Let's see the tone of the following sentences:

- *The Spongebob Squarepants Out Of Water movie is excellent, I loved it!*—The primary tone here is detected as joy.
- *I do think that the part toward the end could be a bit longer, though.*—Here, the Tone Analyzer reports an analytical and tentative tone.

How you can use the Tone Analyzer API

Now, let's take a look at some code. Of course, since there's no training involved, the code is relatively simple.

Let's start off by creating the service instance. Go ahead and create a new **Tone Analyzer** service – I'm sure you remember how, but you can still refer back to Chapter 2, *Can Machines Converse Like Humans?*, if necessary.

There's no tooling since there's no training involved. You're going to be coding all the way! Let's take a look at the following steps:

1. In Python, let's start by importing the Tone Analyzer:

    ```
    from ibm_watson import ToneAnalyzerV3
    ```

2. Next, let's initialize the service class:

    ```
    service = ToneAnalyzerV3(
        iam_apikey="NaPe5R7RNR-e38IRR1jT5k_ictmN1SalGmt64aTC5-f8",
        version="2017-09-21")
    ```

3. Now, let's define some text that you want to find the tone of, and send that through the service:

    ```
    text = "The Tone Analyzer service is very interesting, I hope it
    works."
    service_response = service.tone(
        {'text': text}, 'application/json').get_result()
    ```

   Once you've got that ready, it's time to run your final code.

4. You should see the following output:

```
{u'document_tone': {u'tones': [{u'tone_name': u'Joy', u'score':
0.553157, u'tone_id': u'joy'}, {u'tone_name': u'Analytical',
u'score': 0.87766, u'tone_id': u'analytical'}]}}
```

5. You can then print out a formatted version of that output using the following code:

```
for tone in service_response['document_tone']['tones']:
    print("Tone:\t'" + tone['tone_name'] + "'")
    print("Score:\t" + str(tone['score']), end="\n\n")
```

6. Your output should be as follows:

```
Tone:   'Joy'
Score:  0.553157
Tone:   'Analytical'
Score:  0.87766
```

It's working! Watson provides us with Tone Scores that represent Watson's confidence in that tone prevailing in the text. But that was very simple—how about we do something a bit more complex?

With Watson, you can very easily understand the tone someone is using within a certain passage, but how do you understand a customer's tone within a conversation? You have to take into account what was said before, and how they're reacting to it.

Let's take a look at this conversation, for example:

Customer: Hi. My computer won't turn on. This is really annoying because I just got it 2 weeks ago, and I'm travelling at the moment.

Customer Service Representative (CSR): Hello. I'm sorry to hear you're having this issue. Could I have your computer's serial number?

Customer: Alright, it's [serial].

CSR: Thank you. Could you try running an SMC Reset? Hold down *option, control,* and *command* with the power button until your computer reboots. Ensure it's plugged into power.

Customer: Alright, but you should really make this information more accessible!

Customer: It's working now, thank you!

You could analyze each message individually, but to get a better idea of the customer's tone, you'd need to analyze the whole conversation. To do this, you can actually feed in a JSON object with the conversation into the Tone Analyzer service. Let's take a look at the following step:

1. All you need to do is define this input:

```
utterances = [
  {
    "text": "Hi. My computer won't turn on. This is really annoying
because I just got it 2 weeks ago, and I'm travelling at the
moment.",
    "user": "customer"
  },
  {
    "text": "Hello. I'm sorry to hear you're having this issue.
Could I have your computer's serial number?",
    "user": "agent"
  },
  {
    "text": "Alright, it's [serial].",
    "user": "customer"
  },
  {
    "text": "Thank you. Could you try running an SMC Reset? Hold
down \"option\", \"control\", and \"command\" with the power button
until your computer reboots. Ensure it's plugged into power.",
    "user": "agent"
  },
  {
    "text": "Alright, but you should really make this information
more accessible!",
    "user": "customer"
  },
  {
    "text": "It's working now, thank you!",
    "user": "customer"
  }
]
```

2. After that, simply run the Tone Analyzer:

```
result = service.tone_chat(utterances).get_result()
```

3. When the code is executed, you should see the following output:

```
{u'utterances_tone': [{u'utterance_text': u"Hi. My computer won't
turn on. This is really annoying because I just got it 2 weeks ago,
and I'm travelling at the moment", u'utterance_id': 0, u'tones':
[{u'tone_name': u'Sad', u'score': 0.663713, u'tone_id': u'sad'}]},
{u'utterance_text': u"Hello. I'm sorry to hear you're having this
issue. Could I have your computer's serial number?",
u'utterance_id': 1, u'tones': []}, {u'utterance_text': u"Alright,
it's [serial].", u'utterance_id': 2, u'tones': []},
{u'utterance_text': u'Thank you. Could you try running an SMC
Reset? Hold down "option", "control", and "command" with the power
button until your computer reboots. Ensure it\'s plugged into
power.', u'utterance_id': 3, u'tones': [{u'tone_name': u'Polite',
u'score': 0.909869, u'tone_id': u'polite'}]}, {u'utterance_text':
u'Alright, but you should really make this information more
accessible!', u'utterance_id': 4, u'tones': [{u'tone_name':
u'Excited', u'score': 0.694855, u'tone_id': u'excited'},
{u'tone_name': u'Polite', u'score': 0.609554, u'tone_id':
u'polite'}]}, {u'utterance_text': u"It's working now, thank you!",
u'utterance_id': 5, u'tones': [{u'tone_name': u'Excited', u'score':
0.75465, u'tone_id': u'excited'}, {u'tone_name': u'Polite',
u'score': 0.625227, u'tone_id': u'polite'}, {u'tone_name':
u'Satisfied', u'score': 0.909009, u'tone_id': u'satisfied'}]}]}
```

4. Then, you can format it using the following code:

```
for utterance in result['utterances_tone']:
    print("Utterance: " + utterance['utterance_text'])
    if len(utterance['tones']) == 0:
            print("No tones detected.")
    for tone in utterance['tones']:
            print("Tone: " + tone['tone_name'])
            print("Score: " + str(tone['score']))
    print("\n")
```

And you should get the following output (tabulated for better understanding):

Utterance	Corresponding Tone and Score
Hi. My computer won't turn on. This is really annoying because I just got it 2 weeks ago, and I'm travelling at the moment.	Tone: Sad
Hello. I'm sorry to hear you're having this issue. Could I have your computer's serial number?	No tones detected.
Alright, it's [serial].	No tones detected.

Thank you. Could you try running an SMC Reset? Hold down *option, control,* and *command* with the power button until your computer reboots. Ensure it's plugged into power.	Tone: Polite Score: 0.909869
Alright but you should really make this information more accessible!	Tone: Excited Score: 0.694855 Tone: Polite Score: 0.609554
Its's working now, thank you!	Tone: Excited Score: 0.75465 Tone: Polite Score: 0.625227 Tone: Satisfied Score: 0.909009

You just learned how to get the tone of an entire conversation—and it took no more than a few minutes, thanks to Watson. However, notice that Watson may, in some cases, misinterpret an utterance—when the user talked about making the info more accessible (second from last utterance), that sounds like frustration, not excitement! However, by taking into account the low score of that prediction, and the overall tone of the conversation, you can make a more informed conclusion.

You can now employ this technology in practically any use case that can be augmented by understanding not just *what* someone's saying, but **how** they're saying it. Prime fields to be impacted by this technology will be marketing, sales, customer support, education, and healthcare. I'm sure you've called a customer service helpline before, only to be greeted by a dumb bot that can't help you with your query, only further aggravating your anger and sense of grievance. With the Tone Analyzer, Watson can understand that you're getting upset, and that you should speak to a human.

Understanding personality through natural language

Now, let's move to another interesting topic—that of personality.

With the Watson Personality Insights service, you can garner insight into the personality of anyone by using anything that they wrote. Before we get deeper into this tool, let's take a moment to deconstruct what this means.

Using natural language to infer personality traits

Psychologists have known for a long time that you can infer someone's personality traits based off of the way they write. Not what they write, but how they write. The way you structure your sentences and paragraphs, and the verbiage you choose—these introduce subtle hints or clues as to what certain personality traits of yours could be. As humans, it's very difficult to understand these sorts of patterns, because they're very complex. However, for computers, analyzing millions of sentences and paragraphs to correlate them with personality traits is definitely plausible. Inference can then be done in a very short time—in under a second, in most cases.

Here's a sunburst visualization of Rob and Tanmay's personality:

Here's a text version of the sunburst visualizations above:

Personality Traits	Rob	Tanmay
Adventurousness	(93%)	(95%)
Artistic interests	(50%)	(94%)
Emotionality	(5%)	(54%)
Imagination	(58%)	(88%)
Intellect	(99%)	(100%)
Authority-challenging	(99%)	(100%)
Achievement striving	(87%)	(46%)
Cautiousness	(85%)	(91%)

Dutifulness	(38%)	(57%)
Orderliness	(21%)	(33%)
Self-discipline	(66%)	(27%)
Self-efficacy	(84%)	(52%)
Activity level	(99%)	(68%)
Assertiveness	(95%)	(70%)
Cheerfulness	(7%)	(2%)
Excitement-seeking	(29%)	(21%)
Outgoing	(12%)	(4%)
Gregariousness	(6%)	(0%)
Altruism	(55%)	(72%)
Cooperation	(65%)	(74%)
Modesty	(10%)	(28%)
Uncompromising	(22%)	(58%)
Sympathy	(71%)	(95%)
Trust	(96%)	(55%)
Fiery	(18%)	(25%)
Prone to worry	(24%)	(32%)
Melancholy	(77%)	(76%)
Immoderation	(6%)	(17%)
Self-consciousness	(53%)	(89%)
Susceptible to stress	(28%)	(42%)
Conservation	(0%)	(0%)
Openness to change	(67%)	(60%)
Hedonism	(2%)	(4%)
Self-enhancement	(12%)	(19%)
Self-transcendence	(25%)	(27%)
Challenge	(24%)	(17%)
Closeness	(3%)	(2%)
Curiosity	(74%)	(98%)
Excitement	(26%)	(10%)
Harmony	(1%)	(4%)
Ideal	(12%)	(65%)
Liberty	(30%)	(40%)
Love	(14%)	(14%)
Practicality	(56%)	(32%)
Self-expression	(11%)	(17%)
Stability	(12%)	(12%)
Structure	(71%)	(34%)

The preceding table is an example of how the Watson Personality Insights service works, and you can generate similar charts at the Personality Insights demo page: `https://personality-insights-demo.ng.bluemix.net`.

Personality Insights uses deep neural networks to analyze the way you write to predict your personality traits. It was trained on expert psychologists' analyses of thousands of people, their Twitter profiles, and other literary sources. In the majority of cases, Watson can now do this at near human-level precision, and you can find detailed statistics at: `https://console.bluemix.net/docs/services/personality-insights/science.html#science`.

So, if your friend has a Twitter profile, and you want to figure out what kind of a person they are, you can do so with this service.

Let's take a look at how we can implement this service!

Calling the Personality Insights API

Let's start off with initializing a service instance. Just like the Tone Analyzer, there's no need for the Personality Insights service to have any tooling:

1. We start by importing the API:

```
from ibm_watson import PersonalityInsightsV3
```

2. Then, you simply feed in text after initializing the service:

```
personality_insights = PersonalityInsightsV3(version="2017-10-13",
    iam_apikey="W73kz6O3XR1pkIQVn2RYbrrtIU2o0IvNYuqiMICwSwro")
```

3. Next, create a file called `personality.txt`, a simple text file containing the text from which you wish to infer personality traits. Then, you load the contents of that file into the `profile_text` variable:

```
profile_text = open("personality.txt").read()
```

4. You call the `profile` function on the `personality_insights` instance and call `get_result()` in order to get the JSON output of the service:

```
profile = personality_insights.profile(profile_text,
    "text/plain").get_result()
```

5. You can then format the output nicely using the following code:

```
needs = profile["needs"]
values = profile["values"]
personality = profile["personality"]
def print_traits(traits_category_name, traits):
    print(traits_category_name + ":")
    for trait in traits:
        print(trait["name"] + ":
{:.3f}%".format(trait["percentile"] * 100))
    print("\n")
print_traits("Needs", needs)
print_traits("Values", values)
print_traits("Personality", personality)
```

That's simple, isn't it? This is your final code:

[Chp5-Program-1.py]

```
1.    from ibm_watson import PersonalityInsightsV3
2.
3.    personality_insights = PersonalityInsightsV3(
4.        version='2017-10-13',
5.        iam_apikey='W73kz603XR1pkIQVn2RYbrrtIU2o0IvNYuqiMICwSwro')
6.
7.    profile_text = open("personality.txt").read()
8.    profile = personality_insights.profile(profile_text,
9.            "text/plain").get_result()
10.   needs = profile["needs"]
11.   values = profile["values"]
12.   personality = profile["personality"]
13.
14.   def print_traits(traits_category_name, traits):
15.       print(traits_category_name + ":")
16.       for trait in traits:
17.           print(trait["name"] + ": {:.3f}%".format(
18.                   trait["percentile"] * 100))
19.       print("\n")
20.
21.   print_traits("Needs", needs)
22.   print_traits("Values", values)
23.   print_traits("Personality", personality)
```

If executed, the preceding code should have the following output:

Needs:

```
Challenge: 32.163%
Closeness: 1.031%
Curiosity: 99.248%
Excitement: 4.036%
Harmony: 2.227%
Ideal: 28.864%
Liberty: 32.089%
Love: 10.087%
Practicality: 29.992%
Self-expression: 13.785%
Stability: 1.691%
Structure: 55.492%
```

Values:

```
Conservation: 0.409%
Openness to change: 53.457%
Hedonism: 1.617%
Self-enhancement: 3.480%
Self-transcendence: 31.685%
```

Personality:

```
Openness: 97.723%
Conscientiousness: 47.684%
Extraversion: 13.477%
Agreeableness: 4.298%
Emotional range: 68.415%
```

And just like that, you were able to predict a person's personality traits by using machine learning powered by Watson!

Summary

You've learned how to use **Watson** to simulate a small portion of the human ability of empathy within your applications. You are now able to extract the sentiment of standalone text, and even utterances in conversations! You can also determine personality traits just by analyzing the way someone writes. This means you can now make more informed decisions in all sorts of fields, including recruitment, healthcare, education, security, and more. With this, humans can understand the data that other humans generate at scale, which humans were otherwise incapable of handling, and at the same time, achieve this without letting human bias set us back.

Now that you've got an idea as to how Watson can be implemented to understand natural language, it's time to get to the even more complex APIs: this time, using your own data to train Watson. In the next chapter, you're going to learn how to annotate your own documents to allow natural language analysis to find custom entities in documents that relate to your domain—in this case, finance!

Language - How Watson Deals with NL

6

In this chapter, you're going to learn the inner workings of one of the most complex tasks for machine learning today: language translation! Once you learn the inner workings, you'll be introduced to Watson's Language Translator service, and how Watson's complex technology is wrapped into just a few lines of code for you. Then, you'll be shown how to use the Natural Language Classifier service, which enables you to categorize text into different categories, much like the Visual Recognition service, but for text.

Natural Language Translation is specifically a very difficult task. Let's explore how it's been done in the past!

In this chapter, we will cover the following topics:

- Translating natural languages – the past
- Translating natural languages – the present
- Translating between languages with language translator
- Training custom NMT models with Watson
- Categorizing text using natural language classifier

Natural language translation – the past

Traditionally, **Language Translation** (**LT**) has been a very involved process—people have thought that only humans can really logically translate from one language to another. It requires a uniquely human representation and understanding of the contents of a sentence, paragraph, or document. LT is more than just understanding sentiment—it's about recreating the input data in a different style. It's complex due to the various words, word types, and sentence structures of different languages, and for the following reasons:

- Some words don't have gender attributes
- Some have gender attributes for everything—a *chair* can be masculine or feminine in German
- Most don't have the word *you*
- Most languages, such as French, don't have a literal translation of the English word for *fun*

Therefore, for the past few decades, the majority of research on LT techniques were *best effort*—they'd do word-to-word or phrase-to-phrase translations, but they wouldn't create natural-sounding language.

Not only did they not perform very well, but they required a lot of human input in order to work at all—making it very difficult to scale to, for example, pairs of languages that are rarely translated between say, Welsh and Czech.

So while traditional LT wasn't a very elegant or well-performing solution, it was the best we could do. However, nowadays, there's a new solution! Before we get to that though, let's talk about how we represent natural language in our minds.

Natural language – it's intrinsically unstructured

Natural language is complex because it's a very unique human ability. As humans, when we split from our last common ancestors with chimpanzees (to create the Pan genus (chimpanzees) and Homo genus (humans)), we had to sacrifice our short-term memory ability to make space in our brain for the language center. Evolution proved that it was worth it—with language, we can communicate sophisticated ideas in a concise way to enable very efficient knowledge-transfer among individuals in our species.

As a matter of fact, language is so intertwined in the fundamental working of our brains, that we subconsciously transpose our mental states into language, even if there's no predefined rule for that language. What do I mean?

Well, take a look at the etymology (origin) of the word **pain** from Google Dictionary in the following screenshot:

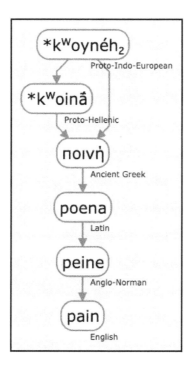

Now, let's take a look at what **poena** meant in Latin.

> *In Roman mythology, Poena (also Poine) is the spirit of punishment and the attendant of punishment to Nemesis, the goddess of divine retribution. The Latin word poena (pain, punishment, or penalty), gave rise to English words such as subpoena and pain.*

Originally, the word *poena* was reserved exclusively for physical pain, in other words, punishment or penalty.

Nowadays, however, we have another kind of pain: mental pain. When did we start to associate that word with both physical and mental pain?

To understand when this association took place, let's take a look at the etymology of the word **sorrow** from Google Dictionary:

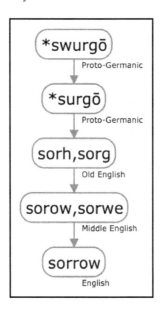

Let's take a deeper look into the meaning of **sorg** from old English. What does this mean? We see grief, regret, trouble, care, pain, and anxiety: Etytree.

There's one key word to focus on there: *pain*. We, at least since Old English, have associated the word *pain* with both mental and physical pain (as indicated by the word sorrow). However, the origin of the word is from physical pain. How did humans make that leap? It's because of the way our brains are structured!

Just a few years ago, it was proven (through MRIs), that just one part of our brain deals with both mental and physical pain (https://www.pnas.org/content/108/15/6270.long). Because the word *poena* was associated, and had a strong physical link, with that pain center of our brain, when humans felt *sorrow*, they'd associate that feeling with that specific word. Eventually, our brains reshaped natural language to fit the structure of our brains.

So, in our brain, the word *pain* has a physical neural pathway to the pain center of our brain. This is how our brains associate complex, abstract mental states in natural language. We can even represent things that we haven't interacted with in any way (seen, smelled, touched, heard, or tasted)—which we now call *imagination*.

Because of the complex way in which the brain represents natural language, translation becomes easy for us. We understand concepts of one natural language by linking them with the relevant clusters of neurons in our brains, and then we convert that specific combination of neural clusters into a different kind of natural language.

Natural language translation – the present

Now, let's get back to LT. Remember, our goal is to create a human-like representation of natural language within computers. How do we do it? Well, let's take a bit of inspiration from the past.

John Rupert Firth was a very famous linguist, and this was one of his most popular quotes:

> *"You may understand a word by the company it keeps."*
>
> *-John Rupert Firth, 1951*

This principle was the inspiration behind enabling **Neural Networks** (**NNs**)to understand natural language. If you can understand the words around a word, you can understand the word itself. What does this mean? Well, with NNs, you can understand words with semantic vector representations of those words. You do this by training neural networks to predict context based off of the word provided.

Take the following sentence:

Tanmay and Rob are writing a book on Watson, a Machine-Learning-as-a-Service platform.

Let's split up the sentence into two different arrays: the input into the Neural Network and the output we expect; so, the following table is the input and output for a simple Skipgram Word2Vec model:

Input	Output
["Tanmay"]	["and", "Rob"]
["and"]	["Tanmay", "Rob", "are"]
["Rob"]	["Tanmay", "and", "are", "writing"]
["are"]	["and", "Rob", "writing", "a"]
["writing"]	["Rob", "are", "a", "book"]
["a"]	["are", "writing", "book", "on"]
["book"]	["writing", "a", "on", "Watson"]
["on"]	["a", "book", "Watson", "a"]
["Watson"]	["book", "on", "a", "Machine"]

["a"]	["on", "Watson", "Machine", "Learning"]
["Machine"]	["Watson", "a", "Learning", "as"]
["Learning"]	["a", "Machine", "as", "a"]
["as"]	["Machine", "Learning", "a", "Service"]
["a"]	["Learning", "as", "Service", "Platform"]
["Service"]	["as", "a", "platform"]
["platform"]	["a", "Service"]

Essentially, we're looping through each word in the sentence. For each word, take *n* words before and after (if *n* aren't available, take as many as possible). In the preceding example, n is 2. The word you chose is the input, the words before and after are the output of the neural network.

If you've worked with machine learning technology before, you're probably thinking, *"Wait a minute! If we're feeding in **a** as an input twice, but with different output, how does the network learn, or, in other words, generalize?"*

That's a great question! the answer? We don't care! To be precise, we don't need the final predictions of the neural network—we need the layer before the predictions.

Before we continue, let's run a quick exercise to understand more about neural networks. For this, you're going to need to install Keras, an open source deep learning library:

```
pip install -U keras tensorflow editdistance
```

(If, on the hardware side, you've got an NVIDIA GPU, and on the software side, if you've installed the WebDrivers, CUDA, and cuDNN, install `tensorflow-gpu`, instead of `tensorflow`, as follows:

```
pip install -U keras tensorflow-gpu editdistance
```

I'm sure you remember how **Convolutional Neural Network**s (**CNNs**) work (from `Chapter 3`, *Computer Vision*). We're going to expand on that knowledge now.

Once a CNN extracts the relevant visual, or spatial, features from an image, it's then the job of the **Multilayer Perceptron Neural Network** (**MLPNN**) to classify those features into a class.

The architecture of the average convolutional neural network for image classification goes a little something like this:

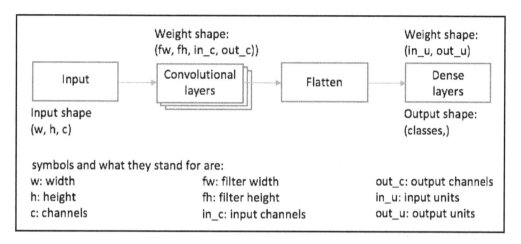

The last dense layer, which represents the output of the neural network, can be called a **logistic classifier**. It enables you to take the features from the second-last layer, and classify them. Think about this: similar images will have similar features abstracted and extracted by the neural network—by extension, similar classes in the logistic classifier layer will have similar weights coming in from the feature layer, which is the second-last layer.

To test this, let's take the ResNet50 (50-layer Residual Convolutional Neural Network) model that's been trained on ImageNet (over 15,000,000 images in over 1,000 categories). If we take a random class, say `Persian Cat`, we should be able to see which other classes the neural network thinks are similar by getting the other classes whose weights have the lowest cosine distance to the one we chose.

To help you do this, I've already put together a little code snipped, called `most_similar_class.py`. You can download it from (https://github.com/PacktPublishing/Cognitive-Computing-with-IBM-Watson/blob/master/Chapter06/most_similar_class.py).

When you run the file, it prompts you for a command. There are two possible commands:

- The `class` command: With this command, you can get the name of a class from its index. For example, `Persian Cat` is at index 283. Therefore, if you were to say `class 283`, it would output `Class: Persian cat`.
- The `similar` command: With this command, you can get the names of the most similar classes from a class index. If you'd like to get the most similar classes to `Persian Cat`, run the `similar 283` command.

Let's take a look at some results of using the `similar` command:

```
similar 283
Classes similar to "Persian cat":
0: Angora, Angora rabbit
1: tabby, tabby cat
2: Shih-Tzu
3: Pekinese, Pekingese, Peke
4: chow, chow chow
```

How about we try `Rotisserie`:

```
similar 766
Classes similar to "rotisserie":
0: microwave, microwave oven
1: butcher shop, meat market
2: space heater
3: Dutch oven
4: hot pot, hotpot
```

As you can see, the model has learned a semantic representation of the concept of a rotisserie, a microwave, a butcher shop, and more. Plus, it's also learned not only about the concepts themselves, but also in which contexts those concepts appear.

Now, let's apply this to natural language!

Let's go back to word vectors. Why don't we care about the final classification layer? Well, let's just say we've got a network with this architecture:

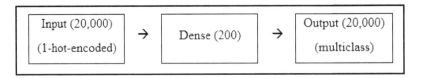

Essentially, we have the neural network take one word out of 20,000 as input, compress it down to a representation only 200 numbers long, and then, using that representation, it predicts, out of 20,000 words, which ones are a part of the context window.

Remember, similar input has similar representations in the second-last layer. Therefore, similar words will have similar vectors in the second-last layer.

This means that you've created vector representations of the semantics of words. Therefore, you can run *arithmetic on words*!

For example, take the vector representation of king, man, and woman, and then run the following operation:

```
X = king - man + woman
```

What should X be? Well, as a human, you should be able to answer Queen. With word vectors, computers can answer this question as well!

Now, let's finally get to the real point of this section: Neural Machine Translation (NMT).

There are lots of ways to do NMT—let me talk about a relative classic. Before that, we have to understand **Recurrent Neural Networks (RNNs)** (yay!).

Recurrent Neural Networks can understand data over time—and natural language is a perfect example of this. For example, the meaning of the last word in the preceding sentence depends on the words that came before it. To understand such temporal relationships, you need RNNs.

 Notice that, with CNNs, you understand spatial relationships, but with RNNs, you understand temporal relationships.

Here's a sketch of a recurrent neural network. In the following example, we understand data over three timesteps, and have, in sequence, two input, two hidden layers, three hidden units in the first layer, one hidden unit in the second layer, and one final output:

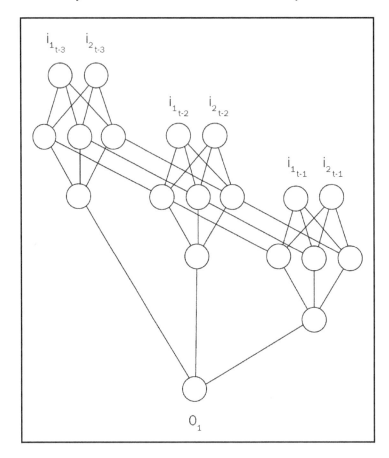

You can probably immediately identify the three main blocks of the neural network. While they were drawn separately in this diagram, they're actually the exact same set of weights and connections. For example, see the connections going from the second layer in the first block to the second layer in the second block? The same weights, or connections, are going from that second layer in the second block to the second layer in the third block. This is a visualization of an unrolled simple recurrent neural network, where the hidden states connect to themselves in the future.

RNNs are trained with **Backpropagation Through Time (BPTT)**.

However, there's one big problem with RNNs: they're very bad at modeling long-term dependencies. If you said something at the beginning of the paragraph, by the time the RNN gets to the end of the paragraph, it's forgotten the beginning. This is where other architectures, such as **Long Short-term Memory Neural Networks** (**LSTMs**) and **Gated Recurrent Units** (**GRUs**), come in.

With these architectures, instead of just adding weights over time, you can selectively choose to remember or forget certain pieces of information. The internal workings of such architectures are outside the scope of this book, but all you need to know is that these architectures work amazingly for NLU (including LT and **Natural Language Classification** (**NLC**)).

Now, let's look at the so-called **classic NMT**—here's the encoder-decoder architecture:

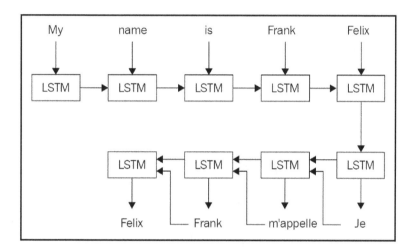

This time, notice that we're using LSTM cells instead of simple RNN cells. In the encoder, each timestep is fed with the next word and the hidden state from the previous timestep. In the decoder, the first timestep is fed with the final hidden state from the encoder, and the rest are fed with that timestep's prediction for a word as well as the previous hidden state from the decoder.

Essentially, this architecture uses an LSTM to encode a sentence into a vector representation, then feeds it into another LSTM to decode that vector representation into another language (in this case, English to French).

Of course, this is a major oversimplification, we didn't talk about the following problems:

- Computational power requirements
- Out-of-vocabulary words
- Sequence lengths

And we didn't talk about these architectures:

- Transformers
- Recurrent attention models
- Quasi Recurrent Neural Networks (QRNNs)
- Temporal convolutions
- Character-level NMT

There's a lot more potential! But for now, let's leverage one of the main advantages of Watson: simplicity. You don't need to worry about architectures. You don't need to know about RNNs, LSTMs, GRUs, word vectors, transformers, QRNNs, attention, or anything else about what goes behind the scenes. Of course, it is fascinating, and helps you to understand how Watson comes to decisions, but Watson is doing the work for you.

Translating between languages with Language Translator

To start, provision a new Language Translator service instance. Once that's done, head over to your favorite text editor, open up a new Python file, and let's get coding:

1. Import the service:

```
from ibm_watson import LanguageTranslatorV3
```

2. Initialize the API:

```
language_translator = LanguageTranslatorV3(version="2018-05-01",
    iam_apikey="rvE894AVGJQ_t_ZNuUoQrclWWQwvpFB0_78jr9pvtjIl")
```

Of course, you will have to use your own API Key.

3. We just need to translate and get our result! But let's make it a bit prettier, and create a command-line interface for it:

```
print("Enter a sentence in English:")
eng_sent = raw_input()
translation = language_translator.translate(
    text=eng_sent, model_id="en-fr").get_result() \
        ["translations"][0]["translation"]
print("Your sentence in French is:\n" + translation)
```

4. Run your code, and let's see some output:

```
Enter a sentence in English:
My name is Frank Felix
Your sentence in French is:
Je m'appelle Frank Felix

Enter a sentence in English:
I shot an elephant in my pyjamas.
Your sentence in French is:
J'ai tiré sur un éléphant dans mon pyjama.
```

That's it! All of the technology that took eight pages of this book to describe on a high level can be implemented in just six lines of code with Watson—but you can take it to another level. How about we train a custom model?

Training custom NMT models with Watson

As you've seen, neural machine translation through Watson is powerful. You're not limited to just word-based or phrase-based translation with Watson. Rather, it tries to understand the true meaning of the input; then, outputs the same intent in another language, even if it has different wording or sentence structuring.

However, natural language is a very broad domain; imagine trying to squeeze the entirety of human language —all of the expressions, vocabulary, domain-specific phrases, and more—into just one dataset and machine learning model. That's, unfortunately, not possible—there are just too many domains and fields, where specific lingo or jargon may be used.

That's why, with Watson, you're not just limited to the pre-trained models—you can train your own models, to tune the language in your own domain!

For example, as you can imagine, the word usage and sentence structure of United Nations speeches are different from the average email. Therefore, it makes sense to train a custom Watson Language Translator model to understand the specificities of the language in the domain of UN speeches.

There are two ways that you can tell Watson how to translate to a different style of language:

- **Dictionary**: Using this method, you explicitly tell Watson which words are converted into which other words in the target language. This isn't very intelligent, but for a lot of cases where certain terminology is required, it works well. For example, in the healthcare domain, there may be certain terminology, such as names of brands, medicine, or diseases, that are translated differently in other languages.
- **Transfer learning**: This technique is more complex, but works very well. It enables Watson to learn how to translate in a way that's so detailed, it even learns differences in sentence structure and phrasing. It requires parallel data, which is essentially showing Watson examples of sentences in the source language and target language. This enables Watson to learn from example.

However, there is one limitation for now: you can't train Watson on a new source-target language pair. For example, from Hindi to Esperanto. Why? Because Watson relies on *transfer learning*.

As mentioned earlier, NMT techniques require a lot of data to train—which sometimes isn't feasible to obtain. So instead of providing the functionality to train brand new models, which would take a lot of time, and tons of resources, Watson supports transfer learning. This allows you to tweak a pre-existing model to better fit your needs.

In this book, we won't get into the technical details of transfer learning or how to create your own custom Watson Language Translator models—but if you need the functionality for more advanced applications, it is available.

Categorizing text using Natural Language Classifier

Now that you've learned how to translate between different natural languages, let's take a look at an example of something that's even simpler: classifying sentences into categories.

For example, let's say that you're trying to analyze the sentiments of people on Twitter. But let's be a bit more specific: you're a data scientist working for an airline, and you want to see how people are reacting to your brand on social media. There are two difficulties here:

- Social media is a complex ecosystem; each platform has its own share of people, often of different demographics, and therefore, a different culture around that platform. On Twitter, you'll see lots of hashtags, people tweeting about things that are trending, abbreviations, and more, that are specific to, or at least most prominent on, the Twitter platform.
- People speak differently about airlines than they do about, say, a grocery store. They use different words, hashtags, and emojis. This is because of both an average demographic change, the expectations of customers will be different, and because of a field change (airlines to grocery stores).

In order to solve both problems at once, you can train a custom Watson model to classify the sentiment of a tweet! By doing this, you're training Watson on both the domain-specific, platform-specific, and demographic-specific lingo that will affect the sentiment classification.

In order to do this, we'll use the `crowdflower/twitter-airline-sentiment` dataset available on Kaggle.

Once you download the CSV file, you'll notice that there's a lot of information present that we don't need. We just require the text of the tweets, and the sentiment classification of the tweets.

You can strip these columns in any way you want—pandas, SFrame, or even opening it up in Excel and removing those columns. Once you've done that, you should have a CSV file that looks like this:

Text	Sentiment
I love Airline!	Positive
I had a bad seatmate on Airline flight.	Neutral
Airline delayed my flight and I missed my job interview!	Negative

There's just one difference: you won't have the column header, that is, the very first header row, in the preceding table.

Once we've got the CSV file ready, we can train the service!

Go ahead and provision TWO services—that's right, two. You're going to provision these services:

- **Natural Language Classifier**: This will help you actually classify your tweets.
- **Cloud Object Storage**: This will be the backend where NLC stores your data and model.

The steps are the same for both services, and they both support a Lite plan:

1. Click on the **Launch Tool** button in the NLC Service that you just provisioned, in order to be greeted by this page:

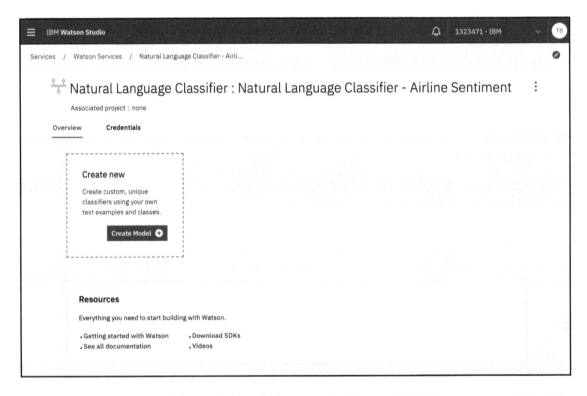

2. Create the model. Do this by clicking on the **Create Model** button toward the left side of the screen. You'll see this page:

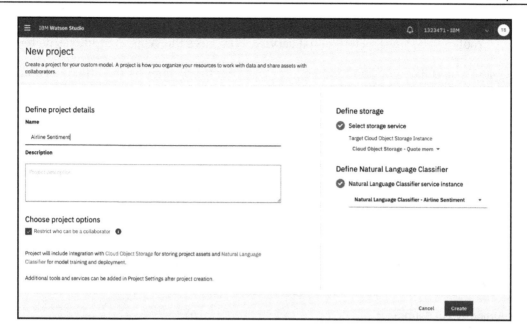

3. Provide your new model with a name, and, if you'd like, a description. On the right, where it says **Select storage service**, select the **Cloud Object Storage** instance you provisioned earlier, as described in the bullet point **Cloud Object Storage** at the start of these steps. Where it says **Define Natural Language Classifier**, choose the NLC service you provisioned earlier, as described in the bullet point **Natural Language Classifer** at the start of these steps. Then, click the **Create** button on the bottom-right. As a result, you'll see this page:

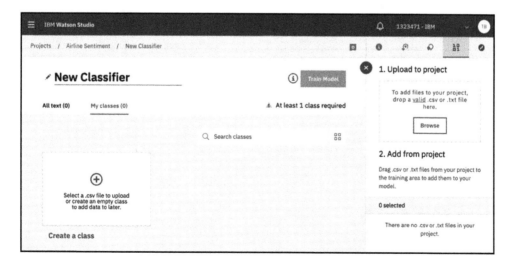

You may remember a very similar page from the Visual Recognition tooling—because, just like that service, NLC uses the Watson Studio as its tooling.

4. If you'd like, you can rename your classifier by clicking on the little pencil on the top left:

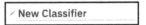

5. Either drag your CSV file onto the **Upload to Project** snippet on the right of the screen, or choose the **Browse** button at the same place in order to choose the CSV file.

6. Drag the CSV file into your service:

7. You should see the classes populate the service. You can now click the **Train Mode**l button on the top-left of your screen and have Watson train the model!

8. This may take up to a few hours, so it's a good idea to keep this running overnight or throughout the day. Once it's done and you're back, you should see this screen when you relaunch the tooling:

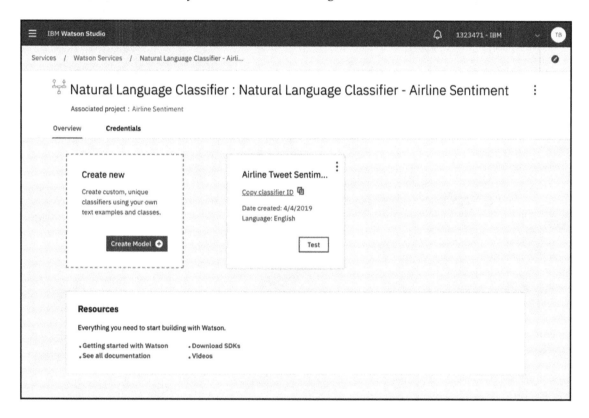

9. That's great! Click the **Test** button on the trained classifier, which should take you here:

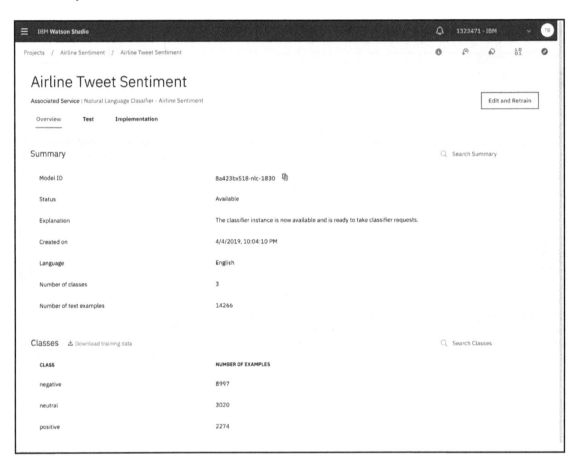

10. Click the **Test** heading on the top-left of the window. You'll see this:

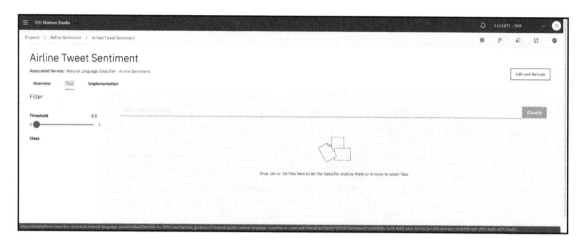

11. You're free to play around with the classifier. Enter a tweet in the textbox, and click on **Classify**. You should see results in the middle of the screen:

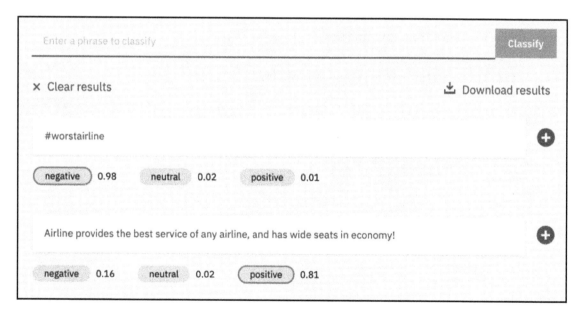

It even understood #worstairline as being negative—wow! #worstairline is just one word, it's not in the English dictionary. Still, using the context from the dataset we provided, Watson understood it as a negative keyword.

Now, let's code this in Python. It's actually quite simple.

The following is a simple Natural Language Classifier JSON retrieval code:

```
[Chp6-Program-1.py]

1.   import json
2.   from ibm_watson import NaturalLanguageClassifierV1
3.
4.   service = NaturalLanguageClassifierV1(
5.       url='https://gateway.watsonplatform.net/natural-language-' + \
6.           'classifier/api',
7.       iam_apikey='JieYHJwBRgrd5Rl9R4q63d5DWvAuffdrRIj1jKhkfoAH')
8.
9.   classes = service.classify('8a423bx518-nlc-1830',
10.        'Airline lost my luggage twice in the same month, delayed ' + \
11.        'my flight, and didn\'t care about my stopover!').get_result()
12.  print(json.dumps(classes, indent=2))
```

All you need to do is import the JSON and NLC libraries, initialize the service instance with your API key, and then get the result of a `classify` call on the RESTful API. Then, you just print the result.

Here's the output I got from my model:

```
{
  "classifier_id": "8a423bx518-nlc-1830",
  "url":
"https://gateway.watsonplatform.net/natural-language-classifier/api/v1/clas
sifiers/8a423bx518-nlc-1830",
  "text": "Airline lost my luggage twice in the same month, delayed my
flight, and didn't care about my stopover!",
  "top_class": "negative",
  "classes": [
    {
      "class_name": "negative",
      "confidence": 0.9157655824185421
    },
    {
      "class_name": "neutral",
      "confidence": 0.07293116018983715
    },
    {
      "class_name": "positive",
      "confidence": 0.011303257391620684
    }
  ]
}
```

Your results may vary, but that's an amazing result! Now, let's make this app a bit prettier by taking user input from the command line, and pretty-print the results:

The following code is the NLC Application, which takes user input and pretty-prints the output:

[Chp6-Program-2.py]

```
1.    import json
2.    from ibm_watson import NaturalLanguageClassifierV1
3.
4.    service = NaturalLanguageClassifierV1(
5.        url='https://gateway.watsonplatform.net/natural-language-' +\
6.            'classifier/api',
7.        iam_apikey='JieYHJwBRgrd5Rl9R4q63d5DWvAuffdrRIj1jKhkfoAH')
8.
9.    user_tweet = input("Give me a tweet: ")
10.   classes = service.classify('8a423bx518-nlc-1830',
11.       user_tweet).get_result()
12.
13.   for sentiment in classes["classes"]:
14.       print(sentiment["class_name"] + " sentiment: " +
15.               str(round(sentiment["confidence"] * 100)) + "% confidence")
```

It's as simple as traversing the JSON that Watson provides. Now, you should be able to analyze the *This airline gave me a free seat upgrade!* tweet:

```
positive sentiment: 99% confidence
negative sentiment: 1% confidence
neutral sentiment: 0% confidence
```

Summary

You did it! You created a custom Natural Language Classifier model using world-class machine learning techniques, which you trained using no code, and tested using just five lines of code.

You not only learned how to use Watson's Language Translator, but also about the technology and algorithms behind it. You also experienced Watson's NLC service with a real, practical example, training it just at the limit of what it's capable of; we fed it roughly 14,000 tweets, and it takes a maximum of 15,000.

In the next chapter, you're going to learn how to use Watson to structure and understand the unstructured, natural-language data your users provide!

Further reading

Here are the links to three papers:

- *Comparative cognitive development*: `https://onlinelibrary.wiley.com/doi/abs/10.1111/j.1467-7687.2007.00570.x`

- *Symbolic representation of number in chimpanzees*: `https://www.sciencedirect.com/science/article/abs/pii/S0959438809000269`

- *Chimpanzees spontaneously take turns in a shared serial ordering task*: `https://www.nature.com/articles/s41598-017-14393-x`

7
Structuring Unstructured Content Through Watson

Since the beginning of the modern computer era, computers have largely been focused on one thing: computing with numbers. Yes, we have had word processors, email applications, and search engines available to us to work on textual information. But in these cases, for those programs, the language of humans is just a collection of words and punctuation, and words are just characters and symbols—in other words, just numbers to the computer.

One of the great breakthroughs that **artificial intelligence (AI)** has brought us is its ability to create a stronger recognition of what people mean when they say things in their own natural language. We call this **natural language understanding (NLU)**.

In this chapter, we will explain the Watson Natural Language Understanding service, along with the Watson Knowledge Studio tool that is used to customize the use of the service.

We will cover the following topics in this chapter:

- Using computers that recognize what you mean
- Introducing the NLU Service
- Customizing NLU
- Using a custom model in NLU

Using computers that recognize what you mean

Have you ever tried to search for something and had trouble finding it? More specifically, have you ever tried to find the one article that you remember reading last year that talked about the impact of how the problems with bundled mortgage loans led to the 2008 global recession—you know, the one that talked about that guy who warned everyone about how bundled mortgages were much riskier than most people thought, but no one listened to him? Try doing a search for that to see how long will it take you to find it. It probably depends on a couple of things: whether you come up with the right set of keywords, how much time it takes to look at different documents, and broken links. What about completely irrelevant information that happened to coincide with the same set of keywords? And that's assuming you even know where to look in the first place – beyond searching the entire internet.

Human language is a tricky thing. Grammatical rules give structure to our language, but the meaning of words is highly contextual, varying dramatically in different contexts. Linguistic devices are leveraged, both formally as well as sometimes wildly, to convey nuance. We use idiomatic conventions to localize and imbue our expression with variety. And, of course, our ability to understand one another rests on the presumption that we share an expansive common history of knowledge and experiences. To decipher the ambiguity of our language, we must at least possess a shared understanding of the basic mechanics of life, psychology, instinctual sensitivities, and social norms.

So, how can we possibly expect a computer to understand our language? What does it possess in the way of any of this shared history? What has a computer gained from exposure to the idiosyncrasies of either formal expression or contemporary convention? What ability does the computer have for adapting to spontaneous experiments in literary form, innuendo, puns, or even complex metaphors? The simple answer is that the computer has no intuitive understanding of human language—or any form of human experience, for that matter. It only knows what has been captured in its machine learning models and other forms of captured logic. It only knows what it has been programmed to know.

We should both draw comfort from this, as well as be awed by the incredible progress that has been made to enable the computer to know even the most basic forms of expressive comprehension. We should be realistic about what the computer can do—knowing that computers are in no way capable of understanding the deeper, more complex forms of reasoning that make us uniquely human. On the other hand, there is a lot that a computer can do by reading and inferring the intended meaning of literary expressions with sufficient accuracy to help us sift through the vast mountains of written information that have been compiled and continue to be expanded every day. It is a tool that can keep us from getting buried in an avalanche of information, and to drill deeply into the core of that information motherload. If information is a resource, and if forms of human expression represent 80% of that resource, and if written language is the majority of that unstructured information, then AI is the refinery that will enable us to process that resource at scale.

To that end, the Watson NLU service is the diamond-tipped drill in our information toolshed.

With NLU, you can use Watson to drill into a single document to understand what concepts are being discussed, what entities are being referred to, and what those entities represent, along with their emotion associated with the expression of that entity; and how those entities relate to one another. You can also see the semantic roles represented in any sentence in the article (subjects, actions, and objects); the keywords found in the article, along with the emotions associated with those keywords; who authored the document and when; and whether the article as a whole is expressing a positive or negative sentiment.

Introducing the NLU service

Let's begin with a basic look at the NLU service and interface.

Like other Watson services, you need to subscribe to the service. For development purposes, you can subscribe to the Lite plan for free. This comes with certain limitations, such as the amount of processing you can do in a given month, and you can only deploy a single custom model per Lite instance at a time (we'll cover customization later in the chapter), but that should be sufficient for most development purposes, and is certainly more than enough for what we cover in this chapter.

You can begin with a simple program, such as this:

[Chp7-Program-1.py]

```
1.    import json
2.    from ibm_watson import NaturalLanguageUnderstandingV1
3.    from ibm_watson.natural_language_understanding_v1 import *
4.
5.    # Create a connection to the NLU service
6.    natural_language_understanding = NaturalLanguageUnderstandingV1(
7.        version='2018-11-16',
8.        iam_apikey='w02JlNpjSbT6OBJSjT1dd3Fe4ebXETJz4yp0etEEFmrU',
9.        url='https://gateway.watsonplatform.net/natural-language-' + \
10.           'understanding/api'
11.   )
12.
13.   # Invoke NLU to analyze the text at the specified URL
14.   response = natural_language_understanding.analyze(
15.       # URL of the page to analyze
16.       url="https://en.wikipedia.org/wiki/SpaceX",
17.       # Indicate what features to find
18.       features=Features(
19.           # Look for up to 4 categories
20.           categories=CategoriesOptions(limit=4),
21.           # Look for up to 10 concepts
22.           concepts=ConceptsOptions(limit=10)
23.       )
24.   ).get_result()    # Get the results of the analysis
25.
26.   print
27.   print("============================================================")
28.   print
29.   print(json.dumps(response, indent=2))
```

Let's examine this code a little closer.

- As we have in other Python programs throughout this book, we begin by importing the `json` library to help us with formatting JSON structures for print purposes on line 1, and we import the `NaturalLanguageUnderstandingV1` package from the Watson SDK library on line 2.
- We will import some specific data-structure object definitions for `Features`, `CategoriesOptions`, and `ConceptOptions`.

Note, that other programs later in this chapter will import additional data structure object definitions, depending on what features are being demonstrated in that program.

- We create a connection to the NLU service on line 6. In this case, we are using an API key to authenticate our use of that service. Don't forget to update the `iam_apikey` with your own API key, which you produced when you created an instance of the NLU service for your own use.
- We invoke the `analyze()` method of the NLU service on line 14.
- On line 16, we specify the web page that we want to analyze.
- Starting on line 18, we indicate what `Features` we want analyzed by the NLU service. In this case, we will be looking for categories and concepts in the document.
- To indicate that we want to see the categories in the document, we create an instance of the `CategoriesOptions` object, specifying, in this case, that we want a maximum of four different categories in the `limit=4` argument on line 20. You can visit `https://cloud.ibm.com/apidocs/natural-language-understanding#text-analytics-features` to learn more about what features are available to analyze, and all of the options that can be specified for each feature.
- We create an instance of the `ConceptsOptions` object, specifying that we want a maximum of 10 concepts from the document on line 22.
- Finally, we print out the JSON object that was returned from the analyze service on line 29.

Note that we are analyzing the internet document at `https://en.wikipedia.org/wiki/SpaceX`. This will produce a JSON data structure that contains the NLU service's understanding of that document, including up to four categories of information and 10 concepts it found in the document.

NLU has a limit of 50,000 characters per document that it will process, so you will also see a warning that this particular document exceeded that limit. You will also see that it recognized that this document was written in **English (en)** and it will report on the number of features and text-units (as calculated in the special way that NLU does that) in the document.

Alternative sources of literature

The program introduced in the *Introducing the Natural Language Understanding service* section had the NLU service examine a web page available on the internet that pertains to **SpaceX**—a company in the private space industry. The source of that page is Wikipedia, which is a non-profit organization and so none of their pages contain advertising. However, it is common for other web pages to contain superfluous information – such as paid advertisements or links to other, sometimes completely unrelated, web pages.

Watson does a good job of stripping out all of this superfluous information from the page before processing it. In that way, it only is processing information that is directly relevant to the core subject of that page.

However, there may be times you want it to consider that other information. You can override NLU by specifying `clean=False` as one of the analyze arguments, like this:

[Chp7-Program-2.py]

```
response = natural_language_understanding.analyze(
        url="https://en.wikipedia.org/wiki/SpaceX",
        features=Features(
                categories=CategoriesOptions(limit=4),
                concepts=ConceptsOptions(limit=10)),
        clean=False
    ).get_result()
```

And what if you want to analyze a document that is not on the web? NLU allows you to process a local document as well by specifying the `html` argument on the `analyze` method, like this:

[Chp7-Program-3.py]

```
response = natural_language_understanding.analyze(
        html="Space/SpaceX and NASA Launch Is First Step to Renewed Human
Spaceflight - The New York Times.html",
        features=Features(
                categories=CategoriesOptions(limit=4),
                concepts=ConceptsOptions(limit=10)),
        clean=False
    ).get_result()
```

Note that the `html` argument takes a file path and name to the HTML file in your file system. At this point, NLU only operates on HTML files. Also note that the `html` argument is a substitute for the `url` argument – you can't specify both.

In addition, you can also process a text string, like this:

[Chp7-Program-4.py]

```
response = natural_language_understanding.analyze(
        text="SpaceX sent the Crew Dragon to various waypoints outside of
the station early Sunday morning, to test the vehicle's docking capability.
Using its onboard thrusters, the capsule periodically approached the ISS
and then held its position over the course of two and a half hours. The
capsule even backed away at one point to test the spacecraft's capability
of retreating in case of an emergency.",
        features=Features(
                categories=CategoriesOptions(limit=4),
                concepts=ConceptsOptions(limit=10))
    ).get_result()
```

In this case, we're using the text argument, and again this cannot be used in combination with either the `url` or `html` arguments.

Types of analyses

In all of these examples, we're only asking NLU to find categories and concepts in the document. But NLU can do so much more. For example, the following use of the analyze method will produce an assessment of categories, concepts, emotion, entities, keywords, metadata, relations, semantic roles, and sentiment, in addition to returning the actual source text that was used in the analysis:

[Chp7-Program-5.py]

```
1.    response = natural_language_understanding.analyze(
2.            url=resource_link,
3.            features=Features(
4.                    categories=CategoriesOptions(limit=10),
5.                    concepts=ConceptsOptions(limit=50),
6.                    emotion=EmotionOptions(document=True),
7.                    entities=EntitiesOptions(limit=100, mentions=True,
8.                            sentiment=True, emotion=True,
9.                            model=Model_key),
10.                   keywords=KeywordsOptions(limit=100, sentiment=True,
11.                           emotion=True),
12.                   metadata=MetadataOptions(),
```

```
13.                    relations=RelationsOptions(),
14.                    semantic_roles=SemanticRolesOptions(limit=50,
15.                            keywords=True, entities=True),
16.                    sentiment=SentimentOptions(['Rockets', 'Space',
17.                            'Mars'])),
18.                return_analyzed_text=True
19.            ).get_result()
```

In order to get this to work, you will have to expand your import statement, as follows:

[Chp7-Program-6.py]

```
1.    from ibm_watson.natural_language_understanding_v1 \
2.        import Features, CategoriesOptions, ConceptsOptions, \
3.            EmotionOptions, EntitiesOptions, KeywordsOptions, \
4.            MetadataOptions, RelationsOptions, SemanticRolesOptions, \
5.            SentimentOptions
```

A full list of the features that Watson can find, and their options, is listed at: https://cloud.ibm.com/apidocs/natural-language-understanding?code=python#text-analytics-features.

Categories

Let's examine each of these elements individually. For the Wikipedia article referenced in Alternative Sources of Literature, NLU found five categories:

```
The following categories of information were found:
    [/automotive and vehicles/vehicle brands] was found, with 84% confidence.
    [/law, govt and politics/armed forces/air force] was found, with 78% confidence.
    [/business and industrial/business operations] was found, with 76% confidence.
    [/technology and computing/internet technology] was found, with 60% confidence.
    [/automotive and vehicles/electric vehicles] was found, with 59% confidence.
```

First, notice that its confidence in these findings is varied. This is an expected characteristic of machine learning – everything is probabilistic, as computed by the algorithm and how well it has been trained to understand the features of that experience.

The categories listed here have a structure: `vehicle brands` is a sub-category of `automotive` and `vehicles`; `air force` is a subcategory of armed forces, which is a sub-category of `law`, `govt` and `politics`, and so forth. This category and sub-category hierarchy was compiled from a very broad analysis of information found on the internet, and is outlined more completely at: `https://console.bluemix.net/docs/services/natural-language-understanding/categories.html#categories-hierarchy`.

You might use this, for example, to determine whether the document is even discussing categories of topics that you care about.

Concepts

The Wikimedia organization has created an open community for crowd-sourcing a consistent ontology of over 4,000,000 things, including over 1,000,000 people, hundreds of thousands of places, creative works, organizations, species, and thousands of diseases. You can learn more about DBpedia at: `https://wiki.dbpedia.org/about`.

Watson NLU is able to identify these concepts and resolve them to DBpedia entities. This is a sampling of the concepts that NLU found in the SpaceX article:

```
The following concepts were discussed:
    [Rocket] with 94% confidence, as identified in http://dbpedia.org/resource/Rocket
    [Falcon 9] with 73% confidence, as identified in http://dbpedia.org/resource/Falcon_9
    [SpaceX] with 67% confidence, as identified in http://dbpedia.org/resource/SpaceX
    [Launch vehicle] with 61% confidence, as identified in
http://dbpedia.org/resource/Launch_vehicle
    [Commercial Orbital Transportation Services] with 57% confidence, as identified in
http://dbpedia.org/resource/Commercial_Orbital_Transportation_Services
    [Space Shuttle] with 56% confidence, as identified in http://dbpedia.org/resource/Space_Shuttle
    [Spacecraft] with 51% confidence, as identified in http://dbpedia.org/resource/Spacecraft
    [Spaceflight] with 48% confidence, as identified in http://dbpedia.org/resource/Spaceflight
    [Launch pad] with 47% confidence, as identified in http://dbpedia.org/resource/Launch_pad
    [SpaceX Dragon] with 47% confidence, as identified in http://dbpedia.org/resource/SpaceX_Dragon
```

The URL for each concept in DBpedia is identified, along with Watson's confidence in its findings, for each concept that it found. You can browse any of those URLs to learn more about that concept. The page for Rocket, for example, looks like this:

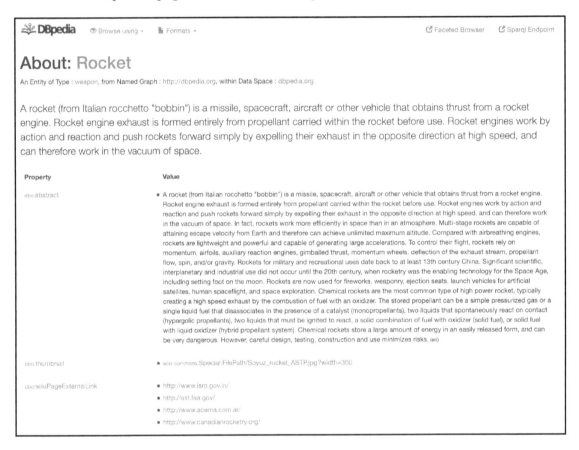

And, of course, any of that information can be navigated programmatically with APIs that are provided by the DBpedia organization, such as SPARQL.

Emotion

NLU will also analyze the overall emotional tone of the document, in addition to the emotional tone associated with individual entities that you care about. In the following example, we can see that the overall tone of the document is primarily joyful, with a little bit of anger, disgust, fear, and sadness.

The overall document had an emotional score of 6% Anger, 5% Disgust, 10% Fear, 50% Joy, and 13% Sadness.

We further asked NLU to evaluate the emotional assessment of Elon Musk, SpaceX, and NASA in this document and got these results. Emotions were assessed for the following target entities:

```
Emotions were assessed for the following target entities:
    [Elon Musk] was assessed with an emotional score of: 9% Anger; 7% Disgust; 62% Fear; 54% Joy; and 14% Sadness.
    [SpaceX] was assessed with an emotional score of: 5% Anger; 8% Disgust; 7% Fear; 56% Joy; and 15% Sadness.
    [NASA] was assessed with an emotional score of: 9% Anger; 8% Disgust; 6% Fear; 50% Joy; and 13% Sadness.
```

Note, that Elon was characterized with both Fear and Joy. This can happen when the same entity is referred to in the document multiple times with different perspectives.

More about the science of emotion detection can be found at `https://console.bluemix.net/docs/services/tone-analyzer/science.html#the-science-behind-the-service` within the Tone Analyzer service that we discussed in an earlier chapter.

Sentiment

The overall tone of the document is represented as a positive, negative, or neutral sentiment evaluation, like this:

```
The overall tone of the document is positive
```

The actual value of the tone is a value between 1 and -1, where any positive value up to 1 is considered a positive tone in the document (by degrees), any negative value is considered a negative tone in the document (also by degrees), and 0 is neutral.

Entities

According to the Oxford Dictionary, an entity is:

A thing with distinct and independent existence. In essence, from a language understanding standpoint, an entity is any noun.

However, NLU attempts to classify entities into types to create a deeper understanding of the thing – not just distinguishing people, places, things, and events, but more specifically whether the person is a corporate officer, a place is a company, a thing is a vehicle, and event is a contract date, and so on.

This is an example of the entities found in the document:

```
The following entities were found:
    [Spacex] of type <Company> was found 152 times, with 92% confidence.
        The entity was found in:
            "Spacex", at index 80
            ...
        The emotional scores for this entity are: 5% Anger; 10% Disgust; 6% Fear; 56% Joy; and 14% Sadness.
        The sentiment score for this entity is: 0.278958
    [CEO Elon Musk] of type <Person> was found 41 times, with 37% confidence.
        The entity was found in:
            "Elon Musk", at index 430
            ...
            "Musk", at index 3361
            ...
            "CEO Elon Musk", at index 5761
            ...
        The emotional scores for this entity are: 0% Anger; 0% Disgust; 0% Fear; 0% Joy; and 0% Sadness.
        The sentiment score for this entity is: 0.0
    [SpaceX Headquarters] of type <Company> was found 2 times, with 31% confidence.
        The entity was found in:
            "the SpaceX headquarters", at index 6584
            "SpaceX Headquarters", at index 28749
        The emotional scores for this entity are: 0% Anger; 0% Disgust; 0% Fear; 0% Joy; and 0% Sadness.
        The sentiment score for this entity is: 0.423723
    [SpaceX] of type <Organization> was found 1 times, with 30% confidence.
        The entity was found in:
            "SpaceX", at index 7994
        The emotional scores for this entity are: 10% Anger; 1% Disgust; 12% Fear; 28% Joy; and 5% Sadness.
        The sentiment score for this entity is: 0.0
    [NASA] of type <Organization> was found 29 times, with 28% confidence.
        The entity was found in:
            "NASA", at index 1402
            ...
        The emotional scores for this entity are: 7% Anger; 7% Disgust; 6% Fear; 53% Joy; and 13% Sadness.
        The sentiment score for this entity is: 0.022774
    [SpaceX Services, Inc.] of type <Company> was found 1 times, with 25% confidence.
        The entity was found in:
            "SpaceX Services, Inc.", at index 27862
        The emotional scores for this entity are: 3% Anger; 18% Disgust; 6% Fear; 4% Joy; and 25% Sadness.
        The sentiment score for this entity is: 0.425099
    [Falcon Heavy] of type <GeographicFeature> was found 11 times, with 23% confidence.
        The entity was found in:
            "Falcon Heavy", at index 1235
            ...
            "the Falcon Heavy", at index 17689
            "The Falcon Heavy", at index 17861
            "their Falcon Heavy", at index 18260
            ...
            "a Falcon Heavy", at index 41317
        The emotional scores for this entity are: 12% Anger; 10% Disgust; 16% Fear; 14% Joy; and 22% Sadness.
        The sentiment score for this entity is: 0.0
    [ISS] of type <Organization> was found 17 times, with 19% confidence.
        The entity was found in:
            "ISS", at index 1362
            "the ISS", at index 1562
            ...
        The emotional scores for this entity are: 2% Anger; 36% Disgust; 1% Fear; 30% Joy; and 34% Sadness.
        The sentiment score for this entity is: 0.0
    [US] of type <Location> was found 13 times, with 19% confidence.
        The entity was found in:
            "US", at index 11049
            ...
            "U.S.", at index 29632
            ...
            "United States", at index 41056
        The emotional scores for this entity are: 9% Anger; 3% Disgust; 13% Fear; 30% Joy; and 15% Sadness.
        The sentiment score for this entity is: -0.272534
```

It is worth noting that Elon Musk was found with three different spellings: `Elon Musk`, `Musk`, and `CEO Elon Musk`. Watson was able to figure out that all three of these spellings were really referring to the same person. Similarly, for `US`, `U.S.`, and `United States`, and some of the other entities that had variations in their spellings.

The ellipses in the listing are to denote that I've removed other entries that are in the actual report generated from my program.

In addition, we can also get the emotional and sentiment scores for each of these entities. These are scored and reported much like the emotion and sentiment for the document overall.

Relations

Relations generally capture the associations that are formed between entities as expressed in the document. For example, the following relationships were found:

```
The following relationships were found:
    A <ownerOf> relationship was found, with 12% confidence, in "This article is about the rocket
manufacturer.", between the following entities:
        within "manufacturer" at index [33, 45]:
            [manufacturer] of type <Organization>
        within "rocket" at index [26, 32]:
            [rocket] of type <Weapon>
    A <locatedAt> relationship was found, with 47% confidence, in "SpaceX's achievements include
the first privately funded liquid-propellant rocket to reach orbit (Falcon 1 in 2008),[12] [note 1]
the first private company to successfully launch, orbit, and recover a spacecraft (Dragon in 2010),
the first private company to send a spacecraft to the International Space Station (Dragon in
2012),[14] the first propulsive landing for an orbital rocket (Falcon 9 in 2015), the first reuse
of an orbital rocket (Falcon 9 in 2017), and the first private company to launch an object into
orbit around the sun (Falcon Heavy's payload of a Tesla Roadster in 2018).", between the following
entities:
        within "company" at index [944, 951]:
            [company] of type <Organization>
        within "International Space Station" at index [980, 1007]:
            [International Space Station] of type <Facility>
    A <hasAttribute> relationship was found, with 70% confidence, in "[85] [86] In July 2017, the
Company raised US$350m at a valuation of US$21 billion.", between the following entities:
        within "Company" at index [11034, 11041]:
            [Company] of type <Organization>
        within "21 billion" at index [11078, 11088]:
            [21 billion] of type <Money>
    A <hasAttribute> relationship was found, with 54% confidence, in "Of this, private equity
provided about $200M, with Musk investing approximately $100M and other investors having put in
about $100M (Founders Fund, Draper Fisher Jurvetson, ...).", between the following entities:
        within "investors" at index [11310, 11319]:
            [investors] of type <Person>
        within "about $100M" at index [11334, 11345]:
            [about $100M] of type <Money>
    A <partOfMany> relationship was found, with 98% confidence, in "Of this, private equity
provided about $200M, with Musk investing approximately $100M and other investors having put in
about $100M (Founders Fund, Draper Fisher Jurvetson, ...).", between the following entities:
        within "Fund" at index [11356, 11360]:
            [Fund] of type <Person>
        within "Founders" at index [11347, 11355]:
            [Founders] of type <Person>
```

This indicates that the manufacturer, of the `Organization` type, is an `ownerOf` (or, in this case, the manufacturer of) a rocket, of weapon type. Watson will indicate the sentence in which the relationship was found, and the index within the document in which the two related entities were found.

Entities and relationships are powerful because from them you can build an ontology for, and more so, a knowledge graph that organizes the information contained in the documents you analyze.

Keywords

Keywords (more accurately key-phrases – as they may contain more than one word) are noun-phrases that appear frequently and prominently in the document. Some people like to think of these as tags that you might use in an internet search to find the document. The following is a sample of the keywords found by NLU in the article:

```
The following keywords were found:
    [Falcon launch vehicle family] was found 1 times, with 69% confidence.
        The emotional scores for this keyword are: 0% Anger; 0% Disgust; 1% Fear; 26% Joy; and 12% Sadness.
        The sentiment score for this keyword is: 0.901006
    [entrepreneur Elon Musk] was found 1 times, with 60% confidence.
        The emotional scores for this keyword are: 4% Anger; 2% Disgust; 7% Fear; 61% Joy; and 1% Sadness.
        The sentiment score for this keyword is: 0.901006
    [maiden launch] was found 2 times, with 58% confidence.
        The emotional scores for this keyword are: 0% Anger; 0% Disgust; 2% Fear; 23% Joy; and 20% Sadness.
        The sentiment score for this keyword is: 0.614473
    [first private company] was found 5 times, with 58% confidence.
        The emotional scores for this keyword are: 0% Anger; 0% Disgust; 1% Fear; 16% Joy; and 2% Sadness.
        The sentiment score for this keyword is: 0.43391
    [rocket manufacturer] was found 1 times, with 58% confidence.
        The emotional scores for this keyword are: 7% Anger; 16% Disgust; 10% Fear; 26% Joy; and 19% Sadness.
        The sentiment score for this keyword is: 0
    [SpaceX's achievements] was found 1 times, with 57% confidence.
        The emotional scores for this keyword are: 0% Anger; 0% Disgust; 0% Fear; 19% Joy; and 2% Sadness.
        The sentiment score for this keyword is: 0
    [Space exploration technologies] was found 1 times, with 57% confidence.
        The emotional scores for this keyword are: 42% Anger; 7% Disgust; 3% Fear; 13% Joy; and 6% Sadness.
        The sentiment score for this keyword is: 0
    [space transportation services company] was found 1 times, with 56% confidence.
        The emotional scores for this keyword are: 17% Anger; 28% Disgust; 2% Fear; 18% Joy; and 8% Sadness.
        The sentiment score for this keyword is: 0.860353
```

In addition, NLU will score the emotion and sentiment that was expressed by the document for each keyword.

Semantic roles

Semantic Roles is an assessment of the object, action, and subject predicates of each sentence in the document. NLU will attempt to determine each of these parts using semantic analysis and will provide alternate interpretations where such variation could exist with the sentence as expressed. Here is an example of this analysis in the SpaceX document:

```
Semantic roles were found in the following sentences:
    "This article is about the rocket manufacturer."
        Subject: "This article".
        Action: "is".
        Object: "about the rocket manufacturer".
    " For the British art gallery, see Spacex (art gallery)."
        Subject: "the British art gallery".
        Action: "see".
        Object: "Spacex (art gallery)".
    " "Space exploration technologies" redirects here."
        Subject: "Space exploration technologies".
        Action: "redirects".
    " Space Exploration Technologies Corp., doing business as SpaceX, is a private American
aerospace manufacturer and space transportation services company headquartered in Hawthorne,
California."
        Subject: "Space Exploration Technologies Corp.".
        Action: "doing".
        Object: "business".
    " Space Exploration Technologies Corp., doing business as SpaceX, is a private American
aerospace manufacturer and space transportation services company headquartered in Hawthorne,
California."
        Subject: "Space Exploration Technologies Corp.".
        Action: "is".
        Object: "a private American aerospace manufacturer and space transportation services
company headquartered in Hawthorne, California".
    " Space Exploration Technologies Corp., doing business as SpaceX, is a private American
aerospace manufacturer and space transportation services company headquartered in Hawthorne,
California."
        Subject: "space transportation services company".
        Action: "headquartered".
```

Notice, that in the sentence `Space Exploration Technologies Corp., doing business as SpaceX, is a private American aerospace manufacturer and space transportation services company headquartered in Hawthorne, California`. A lot is going on. Watson has determined that Space Exploration Technologies is doing business, that it is a private American aerospace manufacturer, and that the space transportation services company is headquartered in Hawthorne, California.

Parts of speech (syntax)

Watson has a new feature of NLU that will return the parts of speech for each sentence in the document as a syntax tree. At the time of writing, this feature is in experimental mode and there is no Python SDK for that feature, but we encourage you to monitor this space for further advances in this service.

The following is an example, as documented on the Watson site, of the JSON structure that could be returned by this service:

```
{
  "usage": {
    "text_units": 1,
    "text_characters": 191,
    "features": 0
  },
  "syntax": {
    "tokens": [
      {
        "text": "Space",
        "part_of_speech": "PROPN",
        "location": [
          0,
          5
        ],
        "lemma": "space"
      },
      {
        "text": "Exploration",
        "part_of_speech": "PROPN",
        "location": [
          6,
          17
        ],
        "lemma": "exploration"
      },
      {
        "text": "Technologies",
        "part_of_speech": "PROPN",
        "location": [
          18,
          30
        ],
        "lemma": "technology"
      },
      ...
      {
        "text": "in",
        "part_of_speech": "ADP",
        "location": [
          165,
          167
        ],
        "lemma": "in"
      },
      {
        "text": "Hawthorne",
        "part_of_speech": "PROPN",
        "location": [
          168,
          177
        ]
      },
      {
        "text": ",",
        "part_of_speech": "PUNCT",
        "location": [
          177,
          178
        ]
      },
      {
        "text": "California",
        "part_of_speech": "PROPN",
        "location": [
          179,
          189
        ]
      },
      {
        "text": ".",
        "part_of_speech": "PUNCT",
        "location": [
          189,
          190
        ]
      }
    ],
    "sentences": [
      {
        "text": "Space Exploration Technologies Corp., doing business as SpaceX, is a private American aerospace manufacturer and space transportation services company headquartered in Hawthorne, California.",
        "location": [
          0,
          190
        ]
      }
    ]
  },
  "language": "en"
}
```

We have truncated the middle portion of the returned JSON for brevity, but there is plenty here to convey the idea of what this service is intended to do.

Customizing NLU

It is remarkable how well Watson performed at assessing this document with its out-of-the-box default model. However, you may have noticed a few things it got wrong. For example, when assessing the types of entities in the document in this summary, the following entities were found:

```
The following entities were found:
    [SpaceX Headquarters] of type <Company> was found 2 times, with 31% confidence.
        The entity was found in:
            "the SpaceX headquarters", at index 6584
            "SpaceX Headquarters", at index 28749
        The emotional scores for this entity are: 0% Anger; 0% Disgust; 0% Fear; 0% Joy; and 0% Sadness.
        The sentiment score for this entity is: 0.423723
    [SpaceX] of type <Organization> was found 1 times, with 30% confidence.
        The entity was found in:
            "SpaceX", at index 7994
        The emotional scores for this entity are: 10% Anger; 1% Disgust; 12% Fear; 28% Joy; and 5% Sadness.
        The sentiment score for this entity is: 0.0
```

SpaceX Headquarters is not really a company, but rather it is a location or perhaps an organizational reference within the company. Likewise, SpaceX is not an organization, but rather the name of the company, also known as Space Exploration Technologies Corp.

Watson is trained from general-domain knowledge. Consequently, it learns about things generically. Anyone familiar with the private space industry would know better about things such as SpaceX. As you specialize the use of Watson, it is likely that you will want to customize its models to the particular domain that you're most interested in. You want Watson to become familiar with the terminology of your domain, the principle types of entities, and their relationships – the information that anyone steeped in that industry would be expected to know.

For this reason, you can train the Watson NLU service to your domain with your subject-matter expertise. This is done using the Watson's Knowledge Studio (be careful not to confuse Watson Knowledge Studio with Watson Studio – they have similar names, and even have some overlapping focus on training Watson machine learning models, but they're not the same tool).

To train Watson on your domain, you will need to annotate some documents from your domain – articles or papers – that demonstrate the use of the lexicon of your industry. The process of annotation is in essence a process by which you create a set of labeled training data. Watson will then learn from that labeled training data what to look for in other text in your domain. It learns what entities are relevant to your industry, their different spellings, how to classify them by their type, and what types of relationships can occur between them.

Preparing to annotate

To perform this task, you will need a set of documents that are representative of your industry. You may have a set of literature that provides a thorough overview of your industry, perhaps even a college text book. It is popular these days to just find a set of internet articles, including recent articles and news reports, that discusses the domain and the key players that you're interested in. For the purposes of this discussion, we have selected a number of internet articles on the topic of the private space industry, with an emphasis on SpaceX.

When using internet content, you have to be mindful of the usage licenses associated with that information. A lot of information on the internet is protected by usage licenses that may or may not allow duplication, republishing, or may have other restrictions.

In the following steps, we will prepare to annotate a set of documents to create label training data:

1. Go to the **AI** Catalog on the IBM Cloud and find the Knowledge Studio service:

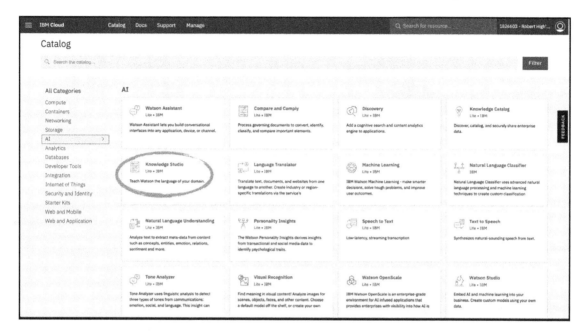

2. Select the **Lite pricing plan** and press **Create**. This will take you to the **Getting Started** page. Select the **Manage** tab, press the **Launch tool** button, then press the **Create Workspace** button to begin the task of annotation:

3. Give your workspace a name, such as **Private Space Industry**, and press the **Create** button:

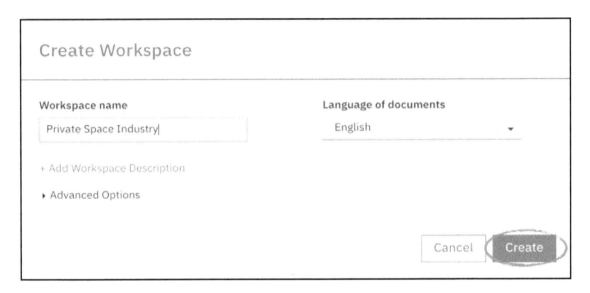

Creating a type system

The first thing you will want to do is create a type-system for your industry, which is a list of common types of things in your industry. In the private space industry, that might include things such as companies, space vehicles, and astronauts. You want to be as complete as you can be. While you can add or change your mind later, doing so may invalidate some of the annotations you made previously and force you to do a lot of rework.

Fortunately, many industries have been creating data models that represent their industries for decades, so you may find one already done for yours as well. Check the Industry Standards Organizations for your domain.

If you don't find one, IBM has curated a general type system from analysis of news articles, known as the **Knowledge from Language Understanding and Extraction (KLUE)**. Sometimes, it's easier to just take that as a starting point, and then adapt it slightly to represent your area of concern, which is what we will do in this case:

1. Go to `https://cloud.ibm.com/docs/services/watson-knowledge-studio?topic=watson-knowledge-studio-typesystem#typesystem` and find the link to the KLUE type system on the page. It should look something like this:

   > A sample type system based on the *KLUE* type system is provided for you
   >
   > Language Understanding and Extraction and was derived by IBM Resea
   >
   > sample KLUE type system from (here)
   >
   > ↗
   >
   > .
   >
   > Many industries, such in domains like metallurgy, geology, market intelli

2. Right-click on the link (the word **here**) in your browser. If you are using Firefox press the **Save Link As...** option, or the equivalent in your browser:

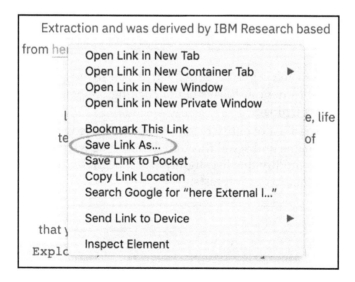

3. Save the `en-klue2-types.json` file somewhere convenient for you.

4. Go back to your **Knowledge Studio** window and press the **Upload** button on the **Entity Types** tab:

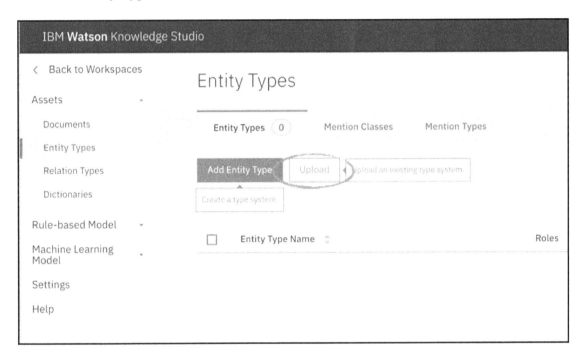

5. Enter the `en-klue2-types.json` file that you saved into to the browser popup by dragging it from your filesystem or clicking on the popup to navigate to it, and then press **Upload**.

6. You should see a list of entity types in your **Knowledge Studio** window. You can sort these by name and scroll through them to see what's there. For this exercise, we're going to modify this list slightly. We'll begin by adding some types that will be important to our interests.

7. Add a **COMPANY** type. Press the **Add Entity Type** button:

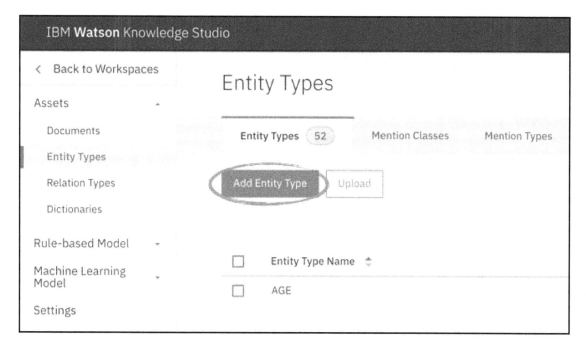

8. Enter COMPANY into the **Entity Type Name** and press **Save**:

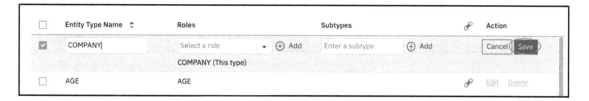

9. Do the same for ASTROBODY, PROGRAM, OFFICER, DAY, CEO, URL, and AMOUNT.

10. Adjust the relationship types. Press the **Relation Types** tab in the sidebar. We're going to add a relationship type that associates `OFFICER as an officerOf a COMPANY`. Press the **Add Relationship Type** button:

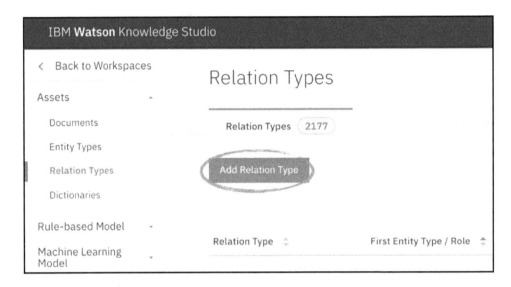

11. Enter `officerOf` as the **Relationship Type**, `OFFICER` as the **First Entity Type**, and `COMPANY` as the **Second Entity Type**, then press **Save**:

You have now set up and modified the type system that Watson will be using for your documents.

Adding documents

Next, we need to sample documents that we can use to train with. As a rule of thumb, you will need at least 10 separate documents. We found some by doing an internet search on `private space industry`. Again, when selecting a document, ensure you have evaluated the license to ensure you have the rights to use it.

We have selected to use an article from MIT News which operates under a `Creative Commons` license.

As an aside

Watson Studio requires that you re-authenticate yourself periodically. If you get a popup that looks like this in the middle of your work, you will have to perform authentication again:

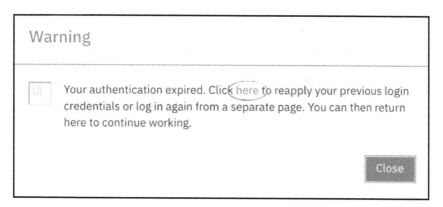

The following are the steps for the watson studio:

1. Press the **Click here** link.
2. This will open a new browser window to allow you to log in, after which it will go to the **Workspaces** page of the studio:

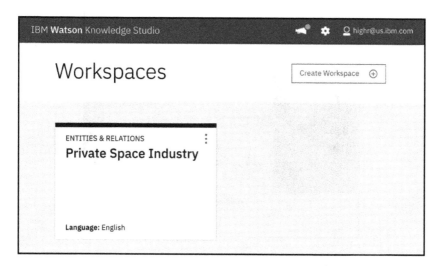

3. Once you've re-authenticated, close that new browser window and resume with the work you were performing in your original window.

4. Return to your original browser window, press the **Close** button on the popup, and continue from where you left off.

5. Occasionally, you will have to repeat the last thing you did when the popup came up, depending on what state the tool was in when it realized you needed to re-authenticate.

Preparing documents for use in Watson Knowledge Studio

Watson Studio can use any of the common document formats, such as HTML, PDF, or Microsoft Word .docx. Since we are using documents obtained from the internet, for our purposes HTML is the easiest.

However, you will want to copy and download the web page in a single (self-contained) HTML file. In your browser, open to the web page you want to use. Now you save that page as a file as follows:

1. In Firefox, the save operation is available under the **File** tab. Press the **Save Page As...** option:

2. Save the file in a convenient location, but ensure you are saving it in the **Web Page, HTML only** format. In Firefox on macOS, it looks like this:

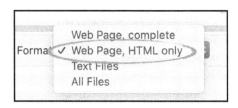

 If you selected the **Web Page, complete** option, Firefox will split the page content into a parent HTML file, with all of its subordinate parts in a sub-folder. That will make it very cumbersome to use in the Watson Knowledge Studio, so you don't want to do that.

3. Do this for 10 documents, but be conscious of the licensing terms for the document.

Loading documents into Watson Studio

You will then have to load the files that you created in the *Preparing documents for use in Watson Knowledge Studio* section into the Studio tool:

1. Go to the **Documents** tab in **Studio** and press the **Upload Document Sets** button:

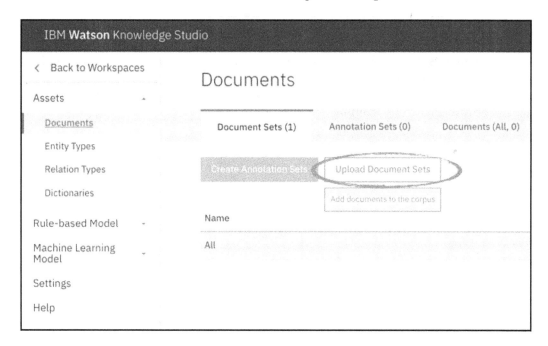

2. Drag your file into the browser popup and press **Upload**, one document at a time:

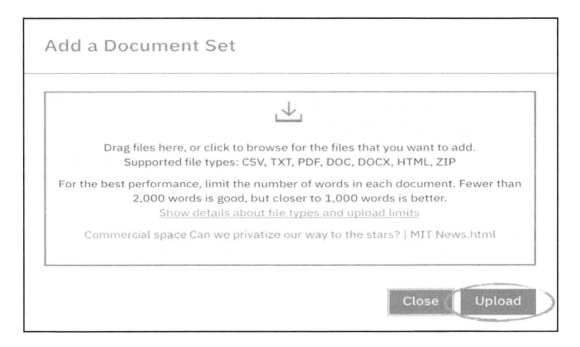

3. You may discover that Watson Knowledge Studio limits the number of characters that can be in a given document. If that is the case, just find another document to use instead. You will find that reasonably short documents are easier to use during the annotation process, and generally are just as good at producing a good training model.

4. Once you've repeated this for all of your documents, you should see a set of these in your **Studio** tool, like this:

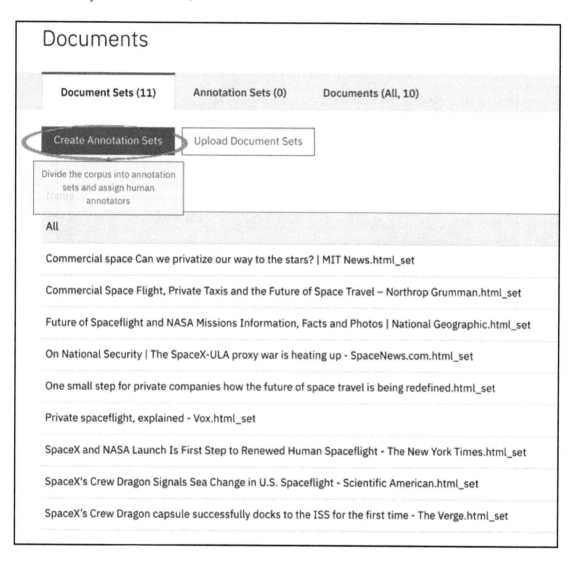

5. Group these documents into an annotation set. Press the **Create Annotation Sets** button. Select **All for the Base set All documents**, **100% Overlap**, select yourself as the **Annotator**, and give the set a name (it is common to just name it after yourself to make it easy to identify in subsequent steps). Press the **Generate** button:

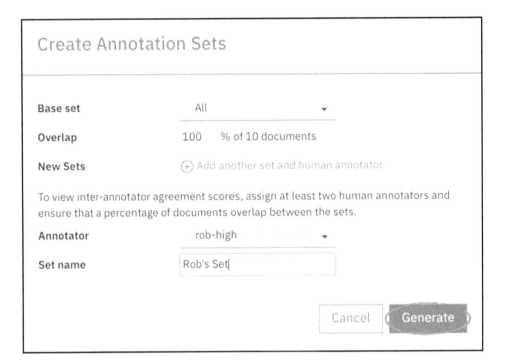

Create Annotation Sets

Base set	All ▾
Overlap	100 % of 10 documents
New Sets	⊕ Add another set and human annotator

To view inter-annotator agreement scores, assign at least two human annotators and ensure that a percentage of documents overlap between the sets.

Annotator	rob-high ▾
Set name	Rob's Set

Cancel   Generate

Performing annotations

Now we're ready to do the real work of annotating these documents (creating labels for the information they contain from which Watson can learn). Follow these steps:

1. Press the **Machine Learning Model** tab in the sidebar to open up additional action tabs, and then press the **Annotation Tasks** tab:

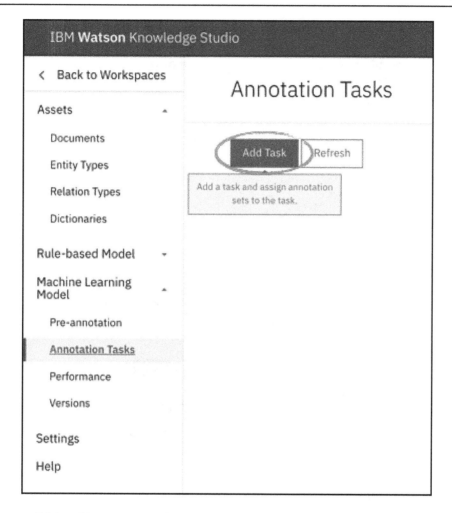

We're skipping over the pre-annotation step—something that you may want to do when you become more comfortable with this process.

Watson Studio centers all annotation work around performing Tasks. You have to create a task in which to do your work. You will see later that this construct is particularly useful for organizing the work of a team of annotators. For now, you will be the only annotator.

2. Press the **Add Task** button. Give the task a name, such as Initial Annotation, and a deadline of today (we're going to be optimistic that you can get through this at this time, but feel free to set it to a couple of days from now if you think you might get interrupted).

3. Press the **Create** button:

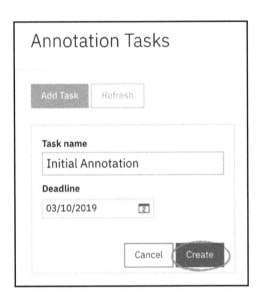

4. Select the **Annotation Set** that you created when you uploaded your documents, and press **Create Task**:

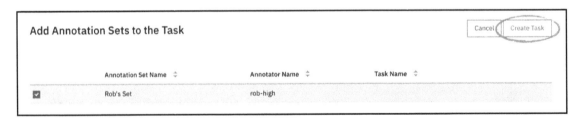

5. Begin that task by pressing on it:

6. Select the **Annotate** button on your **Annotation Set**:

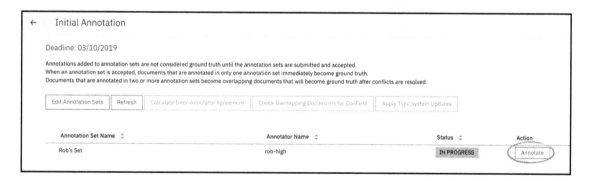

7. Select the first document in your set by pressing the **Open** button:

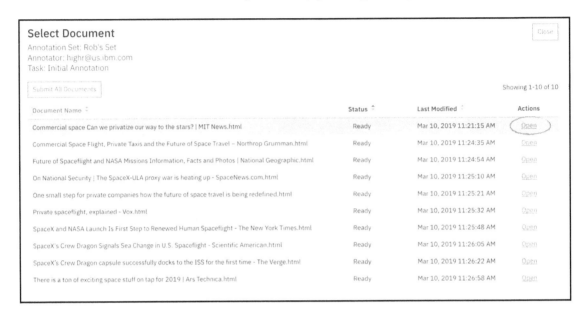

8. The annotation-editing window will open, which will present to you all of the sentences that were found in your document. It may look something like this. On the top-left are the three different editing modes: **Mention**, **Relation**, **Coreference**. We will begin in the **Mention** mode. To the right is a list of all of the entity types in your type system:

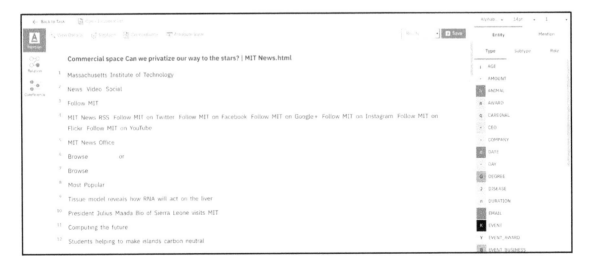

9. Select a bit of text, and label it with its type. You need to be as thorough and accurate as you can be. If you skip a mention, you are in essence teaching Watson how to ignore it. If something is mislabeled, you are confusing Watson about what that thing really is. Let's begin with the first one.

10. Click on the word **Massachusetts** and then expand that selection by clicking on the word **Technology**. This should create a bounding box around the phrase **Massachusetts Institute of Technology**. Scroll through the **Type** list on the right to find **ORGANIZATION**:

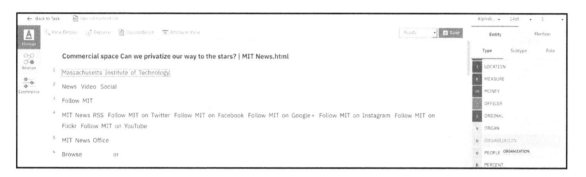

11. Clicking on the **Organization** type will now associate that type with the phrase:

> **Commercial space Can we privatize our way to the stars? | MIT News.html**
>
> 1 Massachusetts Institute of Technology
>
> 2 News Video Social
>
> 3 Follow MIT

12. This can be made even more obvious if you press the **View Details** button at the top of page:

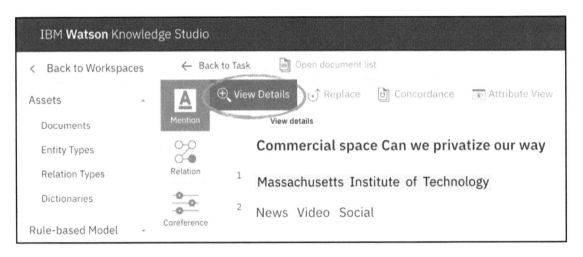

13. The name of the type is revealed above the phrase:

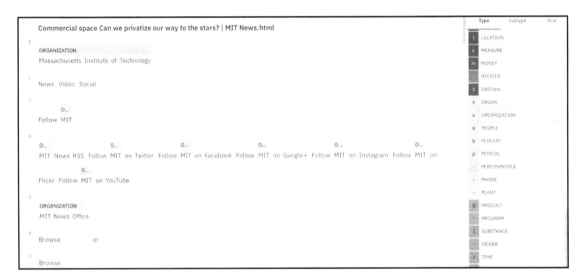

14. Repeat the process of labeling all other mentions to the institute; include other spellings that represent the same entity. Be sure to label them all with the same type, **ORGANIZATION**, in this case.

15. In some cases, you will come across a word that is meaningful, but not important to your area of interest, such as RNA in the following example. You can ignore these; in doing so, you're teaching Watson to ignore them too:

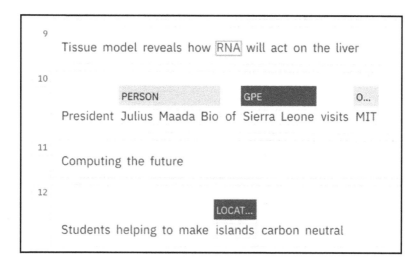

Notice that Sierra Leone is classified as a **GPE**. That stands for **Geo-Political Entity** (shorthand for **COUNTRY** or something similar).

In this example, we've classified the term islands as a **LOCATION**. We could have also classified it as a geological feature, or even a part of a country. Sometimes you will have to use your own judgement on how to classify things, if at all.

Editing the type system

In fact, if you get into this and realize that you are missing key concepts, you can save your work, exit, and go back to the **Entity Types** tab to make corrections to the type system, as follows:

1. Go back to add ELECTED_OFFICIAL to the type system:

Be sure to save your work first!

2. Resume your annotation task by selecting the **Annotation Tasks** tab, and pressing your **Task** card. You will see that your task is **IN PROGRESS**. Before resuming, press the **Apply Type System Updates** button:

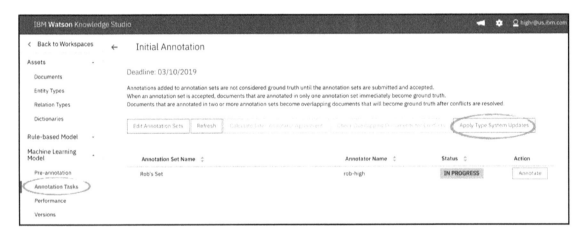

3. This will present a popup asking you to confirm you want to apply these updates because doing so may require you to go back and rework anything you did previously that was affected by the update.

4. Select the document you were working on before by checking your prior work to ensure it is still valid. Assuming you only added a new type, you should be **OK**. You can now classify `President` as a type of `ELECTED_OFFICIAL`:

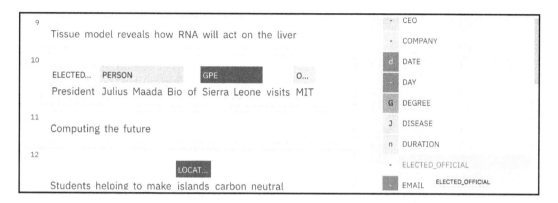

The importance of being thorough

You may notice that the substance of this document doesn't begin to appear until around line 150. This is due to the way this particular page is arranged internally, where a lot of the material at the bottom of the page is actually referenced in the HTML higher in the document. Don't worry about the order of information listed. Watson is more interested in the individual words and phrases, and the structure of individual sentences or passages than the overall structure of the document.

Also, at times, you have to recognize what phrase really represents the thing you are looking for. For example, a date may be somewhat coarse-grained and qualified.

Notice that in the following example we have classified **early 2000s** as a date:

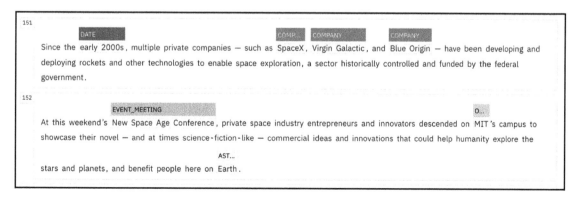

There is a balance between being sufficient and overstating. Generally, you don't want more than a couple of words in your mention of an entity type. But you also need to ensure all the words that are necessary to define that entity are included in the mention. For example, note that **New Space Age Conference** is the entire title of the event and so it has been included in the annotation.

In the end, annotating a document can be a tedious and time-intensive task – especially when you consider that you will need to repeat this for 10 or more documents. Be patient and stick with it. Remember that you are teaching Watson to help you with your other work, and it probably took you a lot longer to learn the subject of your domain.

When you finish this exercise, you will also appreciate why the Knowledge Studio tool is set up to enable collaboration between multiple human annotators – both to help break up the work, and to cross-reference the judgements that different experts might apply to how entities are recognized in the literature. We won't delve further into the collaboration mechanisms provided by the tool at this time, but know they are there, and we encourage you to learn more about them on your own.

Coreferences

The next major task to perform is associating all the mentions that are to the same entity. All of the different spellings of the same thing are call coreferences. You need to identify all of those in your documents. This can only really be done properly after you have finished classifying all of the entity mentions in your document. We'll identify the coreferences using the following instructions:

1. To create a coreference chain (all of the mentions to the same entity) begin by selecting the **Coreference edit** button:

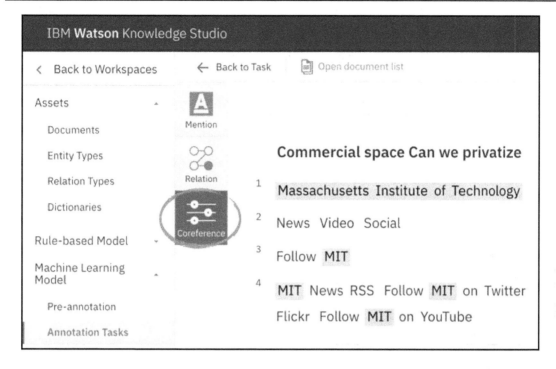

2. Select every mention to the same entity, irrespective of how it is spelled, by clicking on each occurrence. For example, for MIT, we click on each instance of **Massachusetts Institute of Technology**, **MIT**, **MIT Sloan**, and **MIT News Office** (if you agree these all refer to the same organization, which may be a matter of judgement based on what level of organizational granularity is important to your domain):

3. The text you select will be marked with a blue bounding box to indicate it has been added to the coreference chain. Continue selecting all occurrences of these mentions all the way through the document to the bottom:

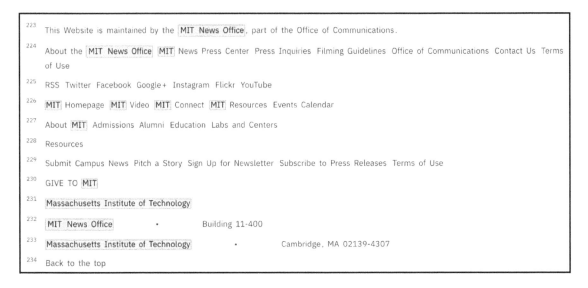

4. At the very last occurrence, double-click the last mention. This will capture the completed chain that is noted in the top-right **Coreference Chains** box:

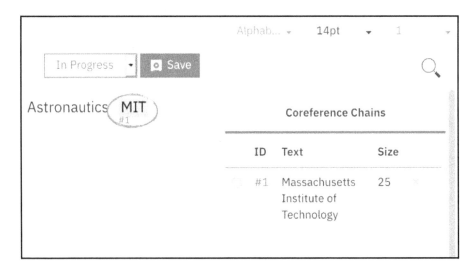

Training Watson

We can now train Watson on our annotations, as follows:

1. Classify all of the mentions in the document that you care about, create all of the coreference chains that pertain to different mentions to the same entity, then save your document.

2. Do the same for all of the other documents in your task.

3. As long as the documents are in the **In Progress** state, you can re-enter the document and continue editing:

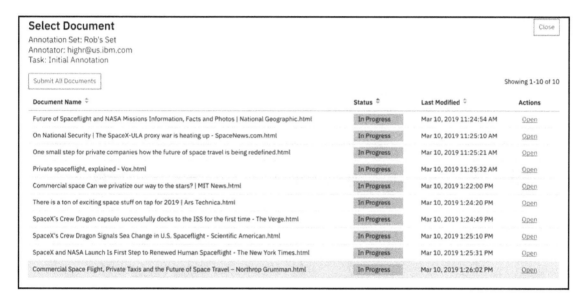

4. Once you are satisfied with your edits, mark them as complete by entering the document and selecting the **Completed** option in the **Save** dropdown, and then press the **Save** button. Alternately, you can submit all of them as completed by pressing the **Submit All Documents** on the document page:

5. Return to tasks, select your **Annotation Set**, press the **Accept** button, and then press **OK** on the confirmation popup (again, these additional steps are there to enable multiple human-annotators to collaborate on a single project, but we're going to ignore that for now):

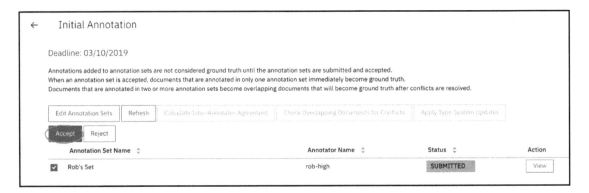

6. Press the **Performance** tab and click the **Train** and **evaluate** button to begin the training process:

7. Ensure **Ratios** for splitting the documents is set to 70% **Training Set**, 23% **Test Set**, and 7% **Blind Set**. This is the recommended default for distributing your training data. The model will be trained with 70% of your training data. It will automatically test the results of that model with 23% of the training data, and finally the blind set will be used to measure the relative accuracy of the training effort.

The test set can be used to assess what you might need to fix to improve the training model's accuracy. You will be able to see these annotations in the evaluation and use that to make improvement decisions.

The blind set will be used again in subsequent training and evaluation cycles so that you can track the progress of your improvements. You will not be able to see these annotations, which will prevent you from being prejudiced by your training improvements.

The following is the image:

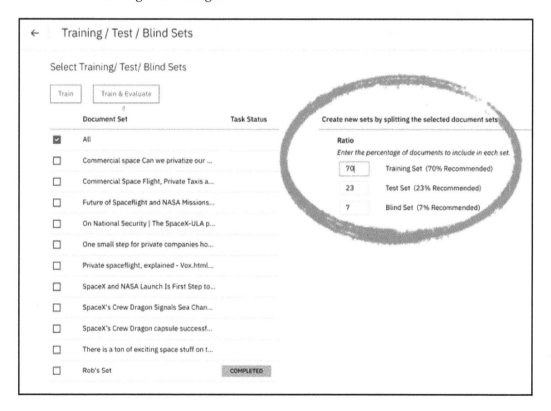

8. Press the **Train & Evaluate** button. This will submit the training job in the background. The progress of that training job will be noted in the upper-right portion of the screen:

9. Training can take several minutes, depending on the complexity of your training data, and the load on the system at the time you initiate the training cycle.

10. When training is complete, you will get an analysis of the model and how well it seems to be performing. In this case, we got an overall accuracy rating of 72%, with a precision of 79% and recall of 66%. That is not bad but could be improved by cleaning up any mistakes we made or mentions that we missed:

11. You can iterate on this process by returning to **Annotation Tasks** tab, repeat the process of creating an annotation task, and further edit the annotations in your documents.

Deploying the custom model to NLU

When training is complete, you can publish your model to NLU:

1. Create a version of this model by pressing the **Create Version** button:

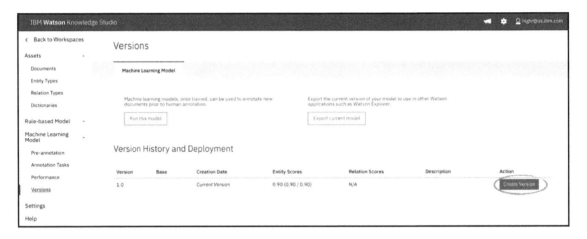

2. Give that a description and then press **OK** in the confirmation popup. This will create a snapshot of the current model, that you can then deploy to NLU by pressing the **Deploy** button:

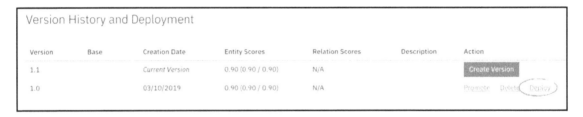

3. You will have to select **Natural Language Understanding** in the popup and press **Next**:

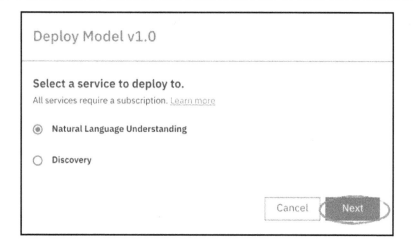

4. In the **Deploy** pop-up, select the **Region**, **Resource Group**, and **Service** name of your NLU instance, and then press **Deploy**:

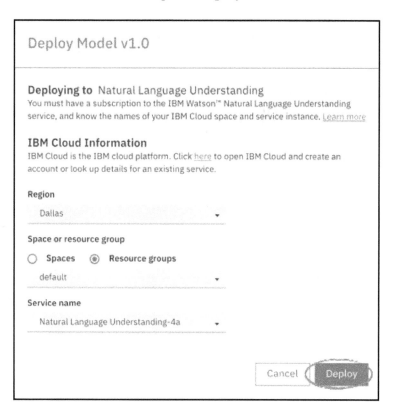

The Lite plans for NLU will only allow you to deploy one model to the instance. If you already have a model deployed to that instance you will have to go into the **Deployed Models** twisty under that version of the model (you will only see that twisty if that model had been previously deployed) and un-deploy it by pressing the **Undeploy** button:

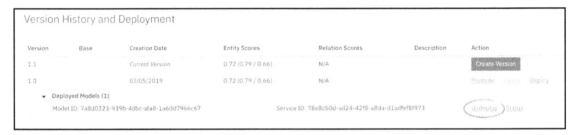

Using a custom model in NLU

Once you have deployed a model to your NLU instance, you can reference that model in the feature attributes for either entities or relations (or both).

The following are the steps:

1. You need the Model ID, which you can get through the `List models` method on the NLU service, or more easily from the **Model ID** listed in the **Version History and Deployment** tab of Knowledge Studio:

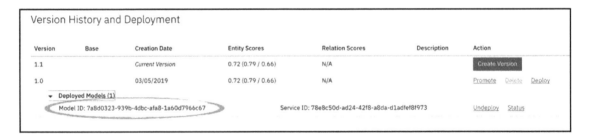

2. Reference that `model` ID in your call to the analyze method:

```
entities=EntitiesOptions(limit=100, mentions=True, sentiment=True,
emotion=True,
    model='7a8d0323-939b-4dbc-afa8-1a60d7966c67')
```

3. When you run the analyze method again with this model, you should see dramatically different results than the entity analysis. It might look something like this:

```
The following entities were found:
    [British] of type <ORGANIZATION> was found 1 times, with 0% confidence.
        The entity was found in:
            "British", at index 55
        The emotional scores for this entity are: 12% Anger; 2% Disgust; 15% Fear; 63% Joy; and 3% Sadness.
        The sentiment score for this entity is: 0.55398
    [Spacex] of type <COMPANY> was found 1 times, with 0% confidence.
        The entity was found in:
            "Spacex", at index 80
        The emotional scores for this entity are: 2% Anger; 13% Disgust; 6% Fear; 31% Joy; and 8% Sadness.
        The sentiment score for this entity is: 0.505617
    [SpaceX] of type <COMPANY> was found 1 times, with 0% confidence.
        The entity was found in:
            "SpaceX", at index 696
        The sentiment score for this entity is: 0.0
    [$2.4 billion] of type <AMOUNT> was found 1 times, with 0% confidence.
        The entity was found in:
            "$2.4 billion", at index 10681
        The emotional scores for this entity are: 4% Anger; 11% Disgust; 33% Fear; 19% Joy; and 43% Sadness.
        The sentiment score for this entity is: -0.307292
        ...
    [Dragon] of type <WEAPON> was found 1 times, with 0% confidence.
        The entity was found in:
            "Dragon", at index 909
        The emotional scores for this entity are: 9% Anger; 7% Disgust; 8% Fear; 18% Joy; and 14% Sadness.
        The sentiment score for this entity is: 0.0
        ...
    [International Space Station] of type <VEHICLE> was found 24 times, with 0% confidence.
        The entity was found in:
            "International Space Station", at index 980
            ...
            "ISS", at index 1362
            ...
        The emotional scores for this entity are: 4% Anger; 4% Disgust; 4% Fear; 19% Joy; and 15% Sadness.
        The sentiment score for this entity is: 0.0321
    [Falcon 9] of type <PRODUCT> was found 1 times, with 0% confidence.
        The entity was found in:
            "Falcon 9", at index 12247
        The emotional scores for this entity are: 5% Anger; 9% Disgust; 6% Fear; 6% Joy; and 4% Sadness.
        The sentiment score for this entity is: 0.0
```

From the preceding sample output, notice the marked improvement in accuracy—SpaceX is recognized as a COMPANY, $2.4 billion is understood as an AMOUNT (of money), and International Space Station and ISS are recognized as being the same thing: a (space) VEHICLE.

Clearly, some additional improvements can still be made. For example, Watson is recognizing Dragon as a WEAPON rather than a VEHICLE or PRODUCT. That may be due to a conflicting annotation. Also notice that Watson has 0% confidence in these assessments. That is likely due to not having enough examples. Ideally, you want close to around 50 mentions of the same entity in your training set for Watson to gain confidence in its training. This can be achieved by adding more documents to your Document Set, annotating them, and retraining the model, as we covered earlier.

Summary

You should now have a good understanding of the power of Watson to understand your literature, how to use the Natural Language Understanding API to get that assessment from Watson, and how to use the Watson Knowledge Studio to build a custom model to help Watson understand the specifics of your domain.

Language is a complex thing. It is full of nuance, subtlety, innuendo, and metaphors. We take that complexity for granted—hardly even thinking about those details as we communicate with each other, especially through the medium of written language. Until now, there hasn't been a good way for a computer to understand any of that about our language. That's not to say that NLU will teach the computer deeper reasoning skills, but it is an enormous leap forward to have it at least recognize the things we say, the variations we may apply to saying them, and to use context to disambiguate different meanings.

In the next chapter, we will bring all of the concepts discussed in this book together into a single, comprehensive sample application. The application will demonstrate how all of the Watson services can be used together to create a truly compelling experience.

8
Putting It All Together with Watson

In this book, we have covered a lot of ground, explaining the fundamentals of Watson's AI services, what they do, how to program them, and how they work. In this chapter, we're going to show you how to bring those services together to build an application. We will construct a functioning application that demonstrates how several of these services can be leveraged to create something of interest, and that should serve as a basis for spurring further ideas and innovation from you as you think about your use of AI in areas that you care about.

In this chapter, we will discuss the following:

- Recapping Watson services
- Building a sample application from Watson services
- Running the application

But, first, let's recap what we learned about those services.

Recapping Watson Services

Watson Services are all available through APIs that you can call from your application. Each of them has been designed to solve specific aspects of recognizing the human experience – whether that's the way we converse, what we see and hear, what we feel, or how we communicate. Watson Services are implemented to perform well out of the box for many general use cases, but all of them can be customized through training techniques to improve their performance in specific situations.

Watson Assistant is useful for creating a conversational flow between users and the computer. This service can be used to create virtual assistants – something that converses with the user to get to the heart of the problem that the user wants to solve. It can classify the user's utterance, extract any entities in that expression, and use that to decide how to respond to the user – perhaps asking further questions to clarify their needs. Remember that a really good conversational system does not simply respond to the user's commands and questions but will delve into the user's own needs to help them figure out what their problem really is.

The **Visual Recognition** service can be used to examine images and videos to classify the objects that are found in them. The Visual Recognition service can recognize different types of objects, locate them within an image, and characterize them. This is useful for situations where you need an extra pair of eyes to monitor things, to help find things, or to sort through a lot of articles – say, on a factory line, or in a warehouse, to find parts, or perhaps in a port,on, allowing users to express themselves to determine the types of cars being unloaded from a ship.

The **Speech to Text** and the complementary **Text to Speech** services enable the computer to hear and understand vocal expressions and to synthesize a vocal response in return. This is useful for any situation where you want to enable interactions with your users without requiring them to use a keyboard and mouse to enter their intentions. The speech services enable a much more natural form of interaction, allowing users to express themselves in a form they're more familiar with and often more comfortable with. As with the other services in the Watson portfolio, the speech services can be trained to recognize and vocalize unusual terms that may be unique to your domain. And the speech synthesis can be tailored to use a variety of voices that may be more appropriate to your circumstances.

The **Personality Insights** and **Tone Analyzer** services enable your computer to build some emotional intelligence so that it is able to recognize the personality of an individual and their emotional tone, based on **psycholinguistics**. Psycholinguistics is the study of determining the personality and emotional state of a person by their expressions, not just *what* they are saying, but *how* they say it. These services can be used to recognize where a user is in their emotional arc, and to tailor the flow of a conversation accordingly, for example.

The **Language Translator** service can be used to translate between different languages – for example, between English and Spanish, French and German, or Arabic and English, and so forth. This is useful when you need to translate documents or passages. In addition, the **Natural Language Classifier** service can be used to recognize the general intention of a document or passage, for example, if you want to quickly summarize what a passage is about so that you can sort through a pile of them quickly.

The **Natural Language Understanding** service can glean a wide range of information from a document, extracting everything from the entities and relationships expressed in that document, determining all of the categories of information and concepts contained in it and the sentiment and semantic roles that it conveys. This is particularly useful when you need a deep summary of an individual document of interest to you.

And, of course, Watson offers several other services that we have not covered in this book. We will discuss those further in `Chapter 9`, *Future – Congnitive Computing and You*, but we encourage you to explore those further on IBM Cloud at `https://cloud.ibm.com/catalog`, to learn more about their utility and use.

Building a sample application from Watson Services

We have built a sample application using most (but not quite all) of the services that we've discussed in the book. Specifically, we have leveraged the following Watson services:

- Watson Assistant (`https://cloud.ibm.com/catalog/services/watson-assistant`)
- Watson Language Translator (`https://cloud.ibm.com/catalog/services/language-translator`)
- Watson Natural Language Understanding (`https://cloud.ibm.com/catalog/services/natural-language-understanding`)

- Watson Personality Insights (`https://cloud.ibm.com/catalog/services/personality-insights`)
- Watson Speech to Text (`https://cloud.ibm.com/catalog/services/speech-to-text`)
- Watson Text to Speech (`https://cloud.ibm.com/catalog/services/text-to-speech`)

This application is functional, but we deliberately kept it simple to stay focused specifically on the programming and use of these services. In that spirit, we have avoided the use of any **Graphical User Interface** (**GUI**), web application, or mobile application front-end, instead opting for a simple terminal interaction.

Like the other sample programs used throughout this book, this sample is written in Python, and should work with either Python 2 or Python 3—although, to be honest, it has only been tested on MacOS.

Note:
You will notice the use of API keys embedded in the program. These API keys are not valid, and you will have to substitute in valid keys that you obtain from your own instances of the services we use in this program.

The use case and application

For this application, we have assumed the following situation. Let's say that you are an investment broker at a bank. You have responsibility for making investment recommendations for your clients. One of the things you need to do is research different companies, the individuals that run those companies, and the general trends in their market—all of which inform your investment decisions. Of course, the internet is a great source of information, but there is a lot of information out there, and you need help navigating that information so that you can distill it down to something useful to you.

In this particular case, we're assuming that you have an interest in the exciting and emerging market of private space exploration – maybe you've heard of the company SpaceX being mentioned in the news, for example. You know of specific websites and internet articles that you want to use as part of that analysis.

This program will allow you to identify a URL of interest and then explore various aspects of the information captured in that article, including who (what entities) is discussed in that article, their personality, and the tone expressed in the article about that person, as well as to get a summary of the article and even translate it into another language.

The entire program is contained within seven program files, which you will find in the resource directories for this book:

- `BankingApp-resesarch.py`: Contains the entry and main program flow for the application
- `TextSpeechService.py`: Contains helper classes for using the Text to Speech service and outputting synthesized speech through the speakers of your computer
- `StreamSpeechService.py`: Contains helper classes for using the Speech to Text service, and getting voice input through the microphone of your computer
- `NLUService.py`: Contains helper classes for using the Natural Language Understanding and the Language Translator services, and processing some of the artifacts that can be obtained from them
- `PersonalityInsightsService.py`: Contains helper classes for the Personality Insights service and generates an attractive form of that analysis
- `TwitterService.py`: Contains helper classes for accessing and getting tweets from Twitter for selected entities
- `skill-InvestmentResearch.20190420a.json`: The Watson Assistant conversational model source used by this program

The program flow

This diagram generally depicts the flow of the program:

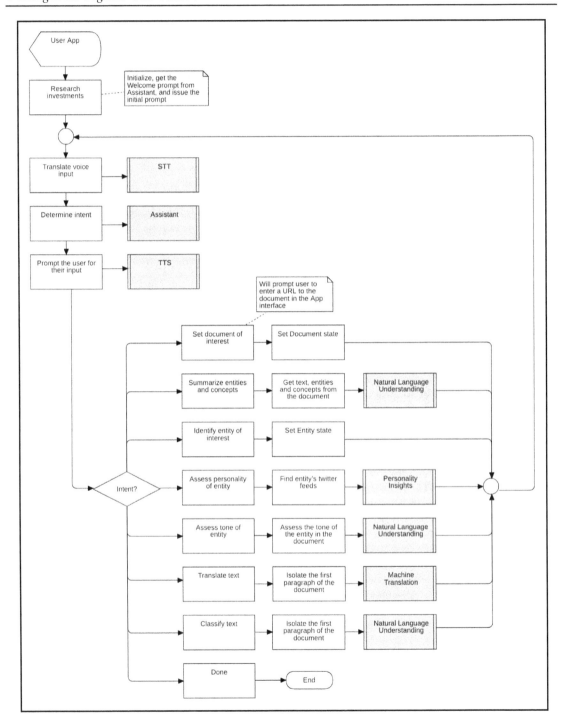

The main program is in `BankingApp-research.py`. It is written in a fairly simple and generic style, prompting for input, and then branching to the logic of specific tasks that need to be performed. After some initial setup, most of the logic is kept within one main loop, which will continue to process until the user asserts that they are done with their research. That main loop begins on line 59 and proceeds all the way down to line 193.

Prior to entering the `main` loop, we initialize the sessions to the various services we depend on, and then we invoke the Assistant, on line 47, to gain an initial prompt for the user, and then speak that prompt to the user.

Then, within the body of the `main` loop, we begin by activating the microphone and transcribing the user's spoken input. We then invoke the Assistant service to classify the intent of their utterance, and determine how best to respond. Next, we select their intent to process that intent. And finally, we return to the top of the main loop to repeat that sequence. We'll break out of that loop when the user expresses their intent to finish.

We kept this inline as much as possible so that you can see the major logic altogether, relying on `helper` classes in the other files primarily just to access the services, or manage the complexities of microphone streams and speaker output, or to access Twitter for the original text, from which we can assess personalities.

This flow has the added advantage that most of the actual interaction flow for the overall dialog is controlled from within the Watson Assistant service. All changes in that interaction, the actual text for that dialog, and any further inquiries that are needed can be controlled primarily through customization in the assistant tooling.

We'll discuss each component of the flow now.

Translating voice input

We need to get input from the user to know what they want to do or ask. With a couple of exceptions, which we'll discuss later, all input from the user is obtained through the microphone, which requires us to use the Speech to Text service to recognize what they said. We specifically use the WebSockets interface of the speech service and stream the microphone input directly to that service through the `PyAudio` package, both of which operate on their own threads, and use an intermediate queue for buffering between the two threads.

The bulk of the speech logic is captured in the `StreamSpeechService.py` program. We won't discuss very many of those details, as the majority of that has already been covered in `Chapter 4`, *This is How Computers Speak*.

From the main program, we create a session to the speech service, and set our preferred voice on line 36:

```
# Create a control object
SPEECH_CONTROL = StreamSpeechControl()
```

This uses a helper class in the `StreamSpeechService.py` program.

We initiate the speech recognition WebSocket on its own thread in lines 38 to 40:

```
# Prepare a thread to recognize the input from the microphone input
recognize_thread = Thread(target=recognizeUsingWebsocket, args=(SPEECH_CONTROL,))
recognize_thread.start()
```

Then, in the main loop, we can turn the microphone on when we want to listen for their input, which we do in line 65:

```
# Get instances of the needed microphone stream
microphoneStream = SPEECH_CONTROL.initAudio()
```

The call to `initAudio()` begins the microphone stream to the `recognize()` service. We then wait until the speech service has heard enough to believe that it recognizes the user's utterance, which we do on lines 67 to 69 by sitting in a loop until the transcription is complete:

```
# Wait for the speech service to transcribe input from the user
while not SPEECH_CONTROL.MYCALLBACK.isTextTranscribed():
    pass
```

With the transcription complete, we can gather the transcribed text from the helper object on line 72:

```
# Process the transcribed input
transcript = SPEECH_CONTROL.MYCALLBACK.getTranscription(True)
```

Once the speech service has done its job, we turn the microphone off to avoid picking up any background noise that isn't relevant to the interaction (including the speaking of the prompt that the program issues through the computer's speakers). We do this on lines 74 and 75:

```
74    # Turn off the microphone while the transcribed text is being processed
75    SPEECH_CONTROL.terminateAudio(microphoneStream)
```

We then echo back what Watson heard the user say and evaluate Watson's confidence in its interpretation of that. If Watson's confidence is too low, then we treat the transcription as garbage so that we can invoke the Assistant service to find out how to prompt the user to provide their input again. All of this happens in lines 77 to 84:

```
77    # Figure out the confidence of the resulting text
78    confidence = int(round(100*transcript[0].get("confidence")))
79    utterance = transcript[0].get("transcript")
80    print("You: " + utterance)
81
82    if confidence < confidence_threshold:
83        print("Watson had poor confidence in what you said.")
84        utterance = "Garbage"
```

The confidence threshold was set on line 34:

```
33    # Prep voice input
34    confidence_threshold = 50    # Watson must be greater than this confidence to accept the voice input
```

You can change that threshold if you find that Watson is doing a better or worse job of understanding your users.

Determining intent

Once we have the user's utterance, we need to determine their intent. We do that by invoking the Assistant service, which takes the user's utterance, classifies it, and, based on the dialog instructions, tells the program what to do next.

Creating a connection to the Assistant service occurs on lines 20 through 24. Notice that we identify the `workspace_id` at this time as well:

```
20    # Create session with the Watson Assistant
21    assistant = ibm_watson.AssistantV1(
22            iam_apikey='PrLJLVykZG4V-FQrADLiZG91oOKcJN0UZWEUAo0HxW8Q',
23            version='2018-09-20')
24    workspace_id = "beb32203-c974-46dd-997f-f91f0968acf5"
```

The primary call to the Assistant to classify the utterance and determine the next response occurs on lines 86 through 95 within the main loop:

```
86        # Invoke Watson to assess the intent of the utterance and determine how
87        # to respond to the user
88        response = assistant.message(
89                workspace_id,
90                input={'text': utterance},
91                context=context).get_result()
92
93        # Get the text and context of the response
94        response_text = response.get("output").get("text")
95        context = response.get("context")
```

In addition to making the call, we also gather the response text and context that the Assistant returned—we'll use those later in the program.

Prompting the user for their input

We generally rely on the conversation model (created with Watson Assistant) to tell us what to prompt for next. Once we have the prompt text, we can use the Text to Speech service to synthesize the prompt, which we can vocalize through the speakers.

 Actually, in this program, we both vocalize the prompt through the speakers and present the prompt text visually in the Terminal window. You could modify that to remove printing to the terminal if you wanted.

To start, we create a session with the Text to Speech service through a helper function in the `TextSpeechService.py` program, which we invoke from lines 29 to 31 of the main program:

```
29      # Prep speech output
30      speechSession = initTextSpeech()
31      voice = 'en-US_AllisonVoice'
```

The prompting is done in two places in the code. We have to do it first before the main loop to initiate the interaction with the user, perhaps with a salutation, and based on what's been directed in the *Welcome* branch of the assistant dialog, which we also call one time prior to the main loop specifically for this purpose. We do this on lines 53 to 55:

```
53      # Display and Say all of the text provided in the prompt
54      for text in prompt:
55          speakAndPrint(text)
```

This code uses the `speakAndPrint()` helper function to both put the text in the terminal window and to initiate the speech synthesis. That help function is captured on lines 16 to 18:

```
16      def speakAndPrint(text):
17          print("Watson: {}".format(text))
18          textSpeech(text=text, voice=voice, session=speechSession)
```

Once we have issued the initial prompt, captured the user's response, and gotten further instructions from the assistant service, we can continue to issue that prompt within the main loop, as we do on lines 99 to 100:

```
98      # Display and Say all of the text provided in the response
99      for text_line in response_text:
100         speakAndPrint(text_line)
```

 Note that the Assistant service can return multiple lines of response and so we place this in a loop to speak and print each line provided.

The actual speech processing is performed in the `textSpeech()` function captured in `TextSpeechService.py`. In that program, we invoke the Text to Speech service's `synthesize()` method to create a wave file of the text prompt on lines 16 through 23. We use a temporary file (called `'glad_to_be_here.wav'` in this program) to hold the results of the synthesized vocalization:

```
16      # Synthesize the expressed text in the indicated voice
17      audio_file=open('glad_to_be_here.wav', 'wb')
18      audio_file.write(
19              session.synthesize(
20                      text,
21                      accept='audio/wav',
22                      voice=voice).get_result().content)
23      audio_file.close()
```

We then use the **PyAudio** package to play that wave file out to the speaker on lines 25 through 39 of that application.

Now that we've gotten the user's input, recognized their intent, prompted them on how the program will proceed and what they can do next, we can now branch on that intent and perform whatever tasks are needed.

Setting the document of interest

If the user indicated they want to focus on a particular document and the Assistant service was able to discern that document from what they said, then we can simply set that document in the state of the program, deriving the document name from the context created by the Assistant service. We do this on lines 113 to 115:

```
113     # Process the #Document-Of-Interest intent
114     elif (response["intents"][0]["intent"] == "Document-Of-Interest") and (context.get("research_document")):
115         document_of_interest = response.get("context").get("research_document")
```

However, typically, these documents are referred to by the URL—something that is hard for the speech service to capture accurately. So, if the Assistant service recognized that the intent of the user's utterance was to do research on a document, but wasn't able to catch the actual document URL, we have provided an alternate way of getting that from the user by prompting them to type it in the terminal window in lines 117 to 133:

```
117     # Process the #Document-Of-Interest intent and prompt for the document URL if needed
118     elif (response["intents"][0]["intent"] == "Document-Of-Interest"):
119         try:
120             research_URL = raw_input("What URL do you want to research? ==> ")
121         except NameError:
122             research_URL = input("What URL do you want to research? ==> ")
123         utterance = "Let's do research on the document at: " + research_URL
124         response = assistant.message(
125                 workspace_id,
126                 input={'text': utterance},
127                 context=context).get_result()
128         # Get the text and context of the response
129         response_text = response.get("output").get("text")
130         context = response.get("context")
131         # Display and Say all of the text provided in the response
132         for text_line in response_text:
133             speakAndPrint(text_line)
```

Note:
Python changed the way that issue prompts for input on the terminal window between Python 2 and Python 3. This difference is accounted for in lines 119 through 122 by first trying it one way, and then trying it the other way if it fails.

To ensure the assistant knows about the entered document, and to give the assistant an opportunity to modify its prompt based on now having set the document URL, we synthesize an utterance made of a set of canned text along with the URL of the document. Note that the assistant is perfectly capable of recognizing a complex URL and capturing that in its context.

Summarizing entities and concepts

If the user asks to summarize the document, and assuming that the document of interest has already been established, we invoke the **Natural Language Understanding** (**NLU**) service to capture the text of the article, the top five entities expressed in the article, and the main concepts that the article is about. We do this in lines 135 through 157:

```
135    # Summarize the document
136    elif (response["intents"][0]["intent"] == "Summarize-Document") and (context.get("research_document")):
137        # Enumerate the article content
138        article_text = getText(research_URL, session=nluSession)
139        print(article_text)
140        # Enumerate the enties found in the document
141        entities = preprocessEntities(getEntities(research_URL, limit=5, session=nluSession))
142        if len(entities) > 0:
143            speakAndPrint("The following entities were found:")
144            text_line = ''
145            for i in range(len(entities)-1):
146                text_line = text_line + entities[i].get("text") + ", "
147            if len(entities) > 1:
148                text_line = text_line + "and "
149                text_line = text_line + entities[len(entities)-1].get("text")
150            speakAndPrint(text_line)
151        else:
152            speakAndPrint("No entites were mentioned in the document")
153        # Enumerate the document categories
154        categories = getCategories(research_URL, session=nluSession)
155        speakAndPrint("The article spoke about these concepts:")
156        for concept in categories:
157            speakAndPrint(concept.get("label"))
```

Lines 137 through 139 get the article text and display it (in unformatted form) in the terminal window. The entities in the document are acquired and then spoken and printed on lines 140 through 150. Or, if no entities were found in the document, that is expressed as well on lines 151 and 152.

Finally, any concepts expressed in the document are acquired and expressed on lines 153 through 157.

Identifying an entity of interest

If the intent is to focus on a specific entity in the document, and assuming the user expressed that particular entity in their utterance, the program will confirm that is an entity that actually exists in the document, and then set that in the state of the program on lines 159 through 161:

```
159    # Process the #Entity-Of-Interest intent
160    elif (response["intents"][0]["intent"] == "Entity-Of-Interest") and (context.get("research_entity")):
161        entity_of_interest = disambiguateEntity(response.get("context").get("research_entity"), entities)
```

If it turns out that the entity of interest does not exist in the document or, more likely, if the entity matches multiple different names, then the `disambiguateEntity()` helper function in `NLUService.py` will prompt the user in the terminal window to supply the correct name.

Assessing the personality of the entity

If the user wants to know about the personality of that entity, the program uses a helper class in **TwitterService.py** to get that entity's tweet history on Twitter and, based on that text, will evaluate their personality. This is performed from lines 163 through 170:

```
163    # Process the #Entity-Personality intent
164    elif response["intents"][0]["intent"] == "Entity-Personality":
165        entity_twitter = entity2twitter(entity_of_interest)
166        if entity_twitter == None:
167            speakAndPrint("Sorry, I couldn't find a twitter handle for " + entity_twitter["text"])
168        else:
169            speakAndPrint("Here's a twitter-based personality analysis for " + entity_twitter["text"])
170            print(prettyPrintProfile(getProfile(tweets(entity_twitter))))
```

If the program cannot find tweets for that entity, it will say so on line 167. Otherwise, the program will assess their personality and present that on the terminal window from line 170.

Assessing the tone of the entity

To get the tone of an entity, the program will use the information captured previously from NLU to get the tone of how that entity is talked about in the document. The previously assessed tone is summarized on lines 172 to 174:

```
172    # Process the #Entity-Tone intent
173    elif response["intents"][0]["intent"] == "Entity-Tone":
174        speakAndPrint("The sentiment of " + entity_of_interest["text"] + " is " +
               entity_of_interest["sentiment"]["label"] + " with an intensity of " +
               str(entity_of_interest["sentiment"]["score"]))
```

This presumes the document has already been identified and summarized.

Translating text

If the user wants to translate the document, the assistant will already have confirmed that they have requested a translation to a valid language. It then gets the document text and then uses a helper class in `LanguageTranslatorService.py` to translate it to the target language on lines 183 to 188:

```
# Process the #Translate-Research intent
elif (response["intents"][0]["intent"] == "Translate-Research") and (context.get("translation_language")):
    article_text = getText(research_URL, session=nluSession)
    translated_article = translate(article_text, response.get("context").get("translation_language"))
    speakAndPrint("I've translated your document to " + context.get("translation_language"))
    print(translated_article)
```

It then presents the translated results in the terminal window on line 188.

Classifying text

Finally, if the user wants to classify the main concepts of the document, the program will get the concepts captured in the document on lines 176 to 181:

```
# Process the #Classify-Text intent
elif response["intents"][0]["intent"] == "Classify-Text":
    categories = getCategories(research_URL, session=nluSession)
    speakAndPrint("The document generally falls into the following categories:")
    for (category_index, category) in enumerate(categories):
        speakAndPrint("Category " + str(category_index) + " : " + category["label"])
```

You might note that this is somewhat redundant to what the summarization intent does. An interesting challenge we leave to the reader is to replace this logic with a call to the Watson **Natural Language Classifier** (**NLC**) service to classify a passage of the document against a set of topics that you are interested in and for which you've trained the NLC service.

Running the program

To run this program, you need to first download the source files, import the dependent packages, and, importantly, create your own instances of the Watson services used by this program. You then need to go into the source files for the program and update them with the API keys for each of your service instances. You can then invoke the program by opening a terminal window, changing to the directory or folder where you downloaded and edited the programs, and then issue the following command if you are using Python 2:

```
python2 BankingApp-research.py
```

Or, if you're using Python 3, then issue the following command:

```
python3 BankingApp-research.py
```

This depends on whether you're using Python 2 or Python 3.

Setup

To set up this application, there are a few things you need to do. In summary, you need to do the following:

1. Install Python, if you haven't already.
2. Download the program files (including the `skill-InvestmentResearch.20190420a.json` file) from the resource `https://github.com/PacktPublishing/Cognitive-Computing-with-IBM-Watson/blob/master/Chapter08/skill-InvestmentResearch.20190420a.json`.
3. Install the dependent packages, including the following ones:

   - `ibm-watson` (`https://github.com/watson-developer-cloud/python-sdk`)
   - `PyAudio` (`https://pypi.org/project/PyAudio/`)
   - `Tweepy` (`https://www.tweepy.org/`)

4. The `ibm-watson` SDK, in turn, has other dependencies that are described in: `https://github.com/watson-developer-cloud/python-sdk#dependencies`.
5. Create your own instances of the Watson services you will use, including the following:

   - Watson Assistant (`https://cloud.ibm.com/catalog/services/watson-assistant`)
   - Watson Language Translator (`https://cloud.ibm.com/catalog/services/language-translator`)
   - Watson Natural Language Understanding (`https://cloud.ibm.com/catalog/services/natural-language-understanding`)
   - Watson Personality Insights (`https://cloud.ibm.com/catalog/services/personality-insights`)
   - Watson Speech to Text (`https://cloud.ibm.com/catalog/services/speech-to-text`)
   - Watson Text to Speech (`https://cloud.ibm.com/catalog/services/text-to-speech`)

6. Update the code to include the `api-keys` for each of your service instances.
7. Create a Watson Assistant workspace by importing the model JSON provided in the `skill-InvestmentResearch.20190420a.json` (https://github.com/PacktPublishing/Cognitive-Computing-with-IBM-Watson/blob/master/Chapter08/skill-InvestmentResearch.20190420a.json) file:

Create Dialog Skill

Create a new skill, start building a skill using the customer care sample, or import an existing skill.

Create skill   **Use sample skill**   Import skill

Select the JSON file for the dialog skill with the data you want to import and choose the artifacts to import to the new skill.

Choose JSON File

⦿ Everything (Intents, Entities, and Dialog)
○ Intents and Entities

Import

See `Chapter 2`, *Can Machines Converse Like Humans?* for more guidance on how to create an assistant workspace.

8. Update the code with your workspace ID as mentioned in the section on *Determining intent* discussed earlier.
9. Once the model has been imported and trained in the Watson Assistant service, you should be all set to run the program.

Have fun!

Summary

In this chapter, we have demonstrated how, with a very modest amount of code, and by leveraging the range of services that Watson offers, you can create something very interesting. Watson's services cover many of the functions that you will need to make an application that interacts with users by voice, that carries on a conversation, that does deep analysis of natural language, that can assess the personalities of key people, and that can translate between different languages. And all of these capabilities can be customized to your own domain through AI training.

The application doesn't have a fancy user interface, and there are plenty of places where the code could be improved, but the core function is a solid representation of what any virtual assistant-like application might look like, and hopefully it will give you a boost when creating your own innovative use of AI. At the very least, this chapter summarized all that we've covered throughout the rest of this book so far.

In the next chapter, we will discuss some general trends and what we can anticipate will happen in the AI industry in the future.

Future - Cognitive Computing and You

9

We have covered a lot of ground on Watson services in this book—everything from how to control a conversation with a user to help them get to their core problems, how to recognize things that can be seen in a camera, or –speech captured by a microphone, through to how to analyze tone and personality in how people write, to classifying utterances, and analyzing the expression of language in documents. Throughout this book, you will have seen that all of these services can be invoked with APIs from your program. Virtually all of these services come with built-in models that are useful right out of the box, but you can always customize them with your own models when you need to adapt them to your problem space.

All the examples that we have used in the book are in English. However, Watson supports many different human languages, and many more are being added all the time—although, which ones these are can vary from service to service. You can always find out the languages that are supported from the service documentation in the IBM Cloud catalog for **artificial intelligence (AI)** services (`https://console.bluemix.net/catalog/?category=ai`).

It is also worth noting that Watson's models are constantly being improved and extended. In fact, it is likely that new features will be added to many of the services that we have covered between the time of writing and when you read this book. We recommend that you return to the catalog frequently to learn about anything new that has been added.

If you run into any problems along the way, you can always get help from the support center at `https://console.bluemix.net/unifiedsupport/supportcenter`. You can get further clarification on support processes at `https://console.bluemix.net/docs/get-support/howtogetsupport.html#getting-customer-support`. Additionally, we highly recommend that you join the Stack Overflow community at `https://stackoverflow.com/questions/tagged/ibm-watson` to find out how other people have solved some of the problems that you may run into.

In this chapter, we will cover the following topics:

- Other services and features of Watson
- The future of Watson
- Advances in AI
- The future of AI

Other services and features of Watson

While we already covered much of Watson's services in this book, there are a number of additional note-worthy services that we didn't. We'll briefly summarize those here.

Compare and Comply

Compare and Comply (**C&C**) is designed to deeply analyze complex business documents that you typically use to govern a business, such as contracts, invoices, and entitlements. It can identify parties, obligations, and the rights that are assigned to each. It can call out contractual clauses such as payment terms, warranties, and liabilities.

In addition to this, the service can be used to compare these elements between two documents—by highlighting the differences between them to assist in quickly understanding what may have changed between two versions of a contract, or how a given contract may differ from a boilerplate contract.

The C&C service can operate on a variety of document formats, including HTML, PDF, TIFF, JPG, and Microsoft Word. It will convert any of these formats to HTML to make it easier to view them in a human-readable form. C&C is also able to do deep analysis of embedded tables, applying semantic interpretation to the cells in a table based on the row and column headers. This ability can also be used to generate a form that can be easily imported into a spreadsheet or relational database table.

C&C does not provide a tool for directly customizing its built-in models. However, it does supply a tool that you can use to highlight inaccuracies in its analysis of your document that then provides feedback to the IBM data scientists for improving the built-in models.

The C&C service can be a great tool for automating governing processes to increase both productivity and reduce business exposure.

Discovery

The Discovery service is the closest thing to what was known as Watson for *Jeopardy!*—that is, the original Watson machine built to answer trivia questions from a large corpus of documents. Discovery can perform a search from either a query (using its special query language) or process a natural-language question. In either case, it will return one or more documents that satisfy this search request, or individual passages that are most likely to directly address the inquiry.

Unlike the machine developed to play the game of *Jeopardy!*, the Discovery service is intended to operate against a corpus of documents that are specific to your domain—for example, the documents that you supply for use within your own instance of the Discovery service. You begin by ingesting your documents into a corpus. Part of that ingestion process includes pre-annotating the document for relevant entities and relationships, which, in turn, speeds up the search process. To do this, the Discovery service builds an internal knowledge graph that you can access for your own application purposes when you subscribe to the advanced or premium plans.

Because Discovery uses entity and relationship classification, it operates in a very similar way to the Watson Natural Language Understanding service—except it's applied to every document in the corpus. Because of this, you can use the Watson Knowledge Studio in the way that we described in `Chapter 7`, *Structuring Unstructured Content Through Watson*, to build a custom model for your particular domain.

Discovery offers three mechanisms for uploading documents into your corpus and activating the ingestion process:

- The first is to use the Discovery tooling to manually add documents.
- Alternatively, you can build a connector to an external document system using the Discovery APIs. Discovery has built-in connector support for Box, Salesforce, Microsoft SharePoint Online or On-Premise, and IBM Cloud Object Storage.
- Discovery also provides a powerful crawler function that will, starting at a root URL that you supply, automatically crawl all of the links it finds in documents at that URL, and then recursively for all of those documents, and so on. This is a great way to pull in an entire website of linked documents. Additionally, you can put the crawler on a cron-job batch-scheduler, such as cron, and it will periodically pull in any changes that were made to that website to help you keep up with ongoing changes. More details are available at `https://www.ostechnix.com/a-beginners-guide-to-cron-jobs/`.

The Discovery service also maintains a special corpus of news data that you can subscribe to—these are news articles that it automatically crawls every day to collect the latest news. You can do inquires against this special corpus to find the news articles that are most relevant to your area of interest.

Watson Studio

Watson Studio (not to be confused with Watson Knowledge Studio) is a whole tool suite and workbench for data scientists. It has several popular open source data science tools built in (including RStudio and Jupyter Notebooks), a very powerful visual modeling tool, and support for common data science languages such as Python, R, and Scala.

With Watson Studio, you can create a community to enable collaboration across teammates. You can build a notebook to progress your analytics work or develop algorithms and models that will assist these analytics. The community is a great way of accessing previously-created content or for posting new content for others to leverage.

 A great video summarizing the capabilities of the Watson Studio community can be found at `https://www.youtube.com/watch?v=jN9vnx5e84A#action=share`.

Machine learning

Along with Watson Studio, the **Watson Machine Learning** (**WML**) service is targeted specifically at developers who want to build their own analytics algorithms and models.

WML is a service that you can access natively, or directly from within Watson Studio. The service is essential for doing machine learning training in the cloud. If you have a training set and machine learning algorithm that you want to train, you can submit a job to the WML service in the background.

As you may be aware by now, training a machine learning model can be very resource-intensive and time-consuming. Even a small model can take minutes to train, while very large models may take hours or even days to complete.

The WML service has at its disposal a large collection of compute resources, which use the latest advances in specialized hardware accelerators, such as **graphics processing units (GPUs)**, for performing the task of training and will schedule the resources needed to perform that task as quickly and as efficiently as possible—therefore, saving you from having to make a big capital investment in machinery that you may only use part of the time. You can find out more at `https://console.bluemix.net/catalog/services/machine-learning`.

Knowledge catalog

Knowledge catalog is a general service for capturing and sharing data across your organization. You can upload datasets and, in doing so, automatically anonymize any sensitive data (the service will substitute an arbitrary token in the place of the original source data) that you want to avoid storing centrally. You can use the service to create summaries that provide a 360-degree view of the information contained in the catalog. Additionally, you can control who is authorized to access the information stored in the catalog.

Watson OpenScale

OpenScale is a product workbench that is used for managing your deployed models—whether these are ones that you are using within any of the other Watson services, or models that you have created for yourself in Watson Studio, or standalone models with WML. OpenScale is designed to let you monitor the performance of your models—including their accuracy and how well they're utilizing compute resources in your production environment.

More importantly, Watson OpenScale will monitor for bias in your models—for example, flagging whether there appears to be a major discrepancy between when the model is flagging for additional fraud-detection among young people versus those in other age categories. This is key to determining whether your models are trained properly to be fair and unbiased to one group or another—whether they are groups of humans, groups of machines, groups of quality categories, or otherwise.

The following video provides a great overview of the key benefits of using OpenScale to monitor for bias in your production system: `https://www.youtube.com/watch?v=6Ei8rPVtCf8#action=share`.

The future of Watson

Over the years, the Watson brand has taken on several meanings. In the beginning, we all knew Watson as the machine that competed against Ken Jennings and Brad Rutter on the US TV game show, *Jeopardy!*. This single event brought more attention to the reawakening of AI than almost any other previous event. It made people across the globe realize that AI had the potential of having a profound impact on our lives. If you're interested in learning more about this project and the significance of the problem that Watson was solving, we highly recommend that you read, *Final Jeopardy: The Story of Watson, the Computer That Will Transform Our World* by Stephan Baker (ISBN-13: 978-0547747194).

Since then, the core functionalities that made up this project were transformed into a set of services available as cloud APIs—which are the primary focus of this book. However, not long after, IBM created a separate business unit to advance the application of these AI technologies within the healthcare domain—which is now known as `Watson Health`. This business has dramatically accelerated the benefit of AI for various tasks such as helping doctors identify the appropriate treatment for their cancer patients. This is now being expanded to other chronic diseases. In addition to this, the Watson healthcare business is applying AI to help doctors interpret various medical images—including x-rays, MRIs, and CT scans.

This success has spawned other industry-specific business units, such as the Watson IoT business (which is focused on bringing analytics to the task of asset management, quality insights, and worker insights), Watson Talent (which is focused on the task of finding and growing the talent in your business), Watson Advertising, Watson Commerce, Watson Education, Watson Financial Services, Watson Marketing, Watson Supply Chain, and Watson Work.

Additionally, IBM has invested significantly in the research of AI and has become one of the largest sources of papers on AI, and not to mention leading the industry in AI patenting. You can read more about the work that IBM Research is doing here: `https://www.research.ibm.com/artificial-intelligence/`. In particular, we encourage you to peruse the wealth of publications that are cataloged by IBM at `https://www.research.ibm.com/artificial-intelligence/publications/`.

The authors of this book are in no position to make commitments for IBM, but it is reasonable to speculate that IBM will continue to advance Watson in three main ways:

- By continuing to refine the science of AI technologies, and apply these to their existing services and solution offerings

- By adding new service APIs for new aspects of AI, including those spun out of the science being created by the IBM Research division
- By entering into new industry-specific vertical domains with solutions to address specific needs in those areas

Advances in AI

Much of the larger and more profound impact that AI will have on our world is in the distant future. But we are seeing an incredible array of advances in technology occurring now—some of which will prove useful, and others, perhaps, not so much. Let's touch on a few of the more promising ones here.

Generative adversarial networks

One of the more interesting advances in recent years has been the introduction of generative adversarial networks. The principle behind this technology is fairly straightforward: two algorithms are developed.

The first algorithm is designed to generate a thing—this can be anything, such as a picture of a cat. Obviously, without having first been taught how to generate a picture of a cat the algorithm just generates some random image that it presents as a cat.

The second algorithm has been trained to recognize that thing—such as a picture of a cat in this example.

The two algorithms are then hooked together, with the first algorithm generating pictures of cats, and the second algorithm judging whether what the first algorithm created actually looked like a cat. The output of the judgment is fed back into the first algorithm, which is responsible for creating pictures of cats.

This process of generating, judging, and learning is put on a continuous loop until the generation of cat pictures is perfected—essentially teaching the first algorithm to create really good pictures of cats.

This technique was recently used to teach an algorithm to create a photo-realistic fake picture of a person—this is a potentially scary thought, but it is also intriguing when you think of the potential for AI to generate new ideas in a domain of your interest.

Conversational systems

Most conversational systems are geared to a paradigm of dialog-flow construction. While some of these, such as the Watson Assistant service that we discussed in `Chapter 2`, *Can Machines Converse Like Humans?*, are richer than others, they are still geared towards conversations that are controlled by the agent, rather than the human. Under normal human-to-human conversations, the flow can be controlled by either party and often, the command of control will swap back and forth over the course of the conversation.

Additionally, the conversation is informed by both shared history and a deep perception of each other's context. Even mundane things, such as both people being in the same room, being exposed to the ambient temperature of the room, the interference of outside noises, or the direction of sunlight, can have a bearing on the conversation. If one party is uncomfortable, then the other party, noticing this, may change their conversational approach to compensate for that discomfort—by using shorter sentences, for example. Alternatively, if a loud noise interrupts the speaker's train of thought, the listener will understand this and accommodate a reset in the conversation.

And, of course, this depth of perception can aid in other ways. For example, if one party doesn't really know the other party, but saw them earlier and perhaps had a brief exchange; this sense of familiarity can lead to a more relaxed discussion, even without being formally introduced. Or, if seeing a client holding a check, a teller can use this context when the client says *"I want to make a deposit"*, and assume that they meant to deposit a check —therefore, filling in the gaps to understand their intent without everything having to be so explicit.

Finally, there are many ways of expressing an idea, and the form of expression should coincide with the context of the conversation. The conversational agent must be able to generate a form of natural-language expression for their part in the conversation that is contextually relevant.

All of these advances are likely to make their way into the market over the next few years, thereby making conversational systems even more valuable for customer care and support. Already this year, we have seen numerous papers published on topics ranging from understanding antecedents and consequences (`https://link.springer.com/chapter/10.1007/978-3-319-98512-1_5`), task-oriented versus social-oriented conversational assistants, and a deep analysis of good conversational design. This is an area that is clearly undergoing a tremendous amount of innovation and is likely to evolve rapidly.

Deep learning

Deep learning (**DL**), also known as neural networks, has become the mainstay of most of the research in AI. DL has the benefit of learning its own features and is, therefore, able to increase the accuracy of its results over other more traditional approaches such as **Logistical Regression** (**LR**) and **Support Vector Machines** (**SVMs**), which require human-engineered features. However, DL has the disadvantage of requiring a great deal more training data to reach these lofty accuracy goals. Finding or creating training data for DL can be time-consuming, labor-intensive, expensive, and, sometimes, just down-right limiting. For example, it is very difficult to train speech-recognition systems that work well for children. Why? Because there are numerous child-safety regulations that restrict you from recording them—not to mention that it can be difficult sometimes to get kids to do what you need them to do.

DL has also been the target of several attacks that undermine the integrity of the algorithms. For example, it has been demonstrated that a picture can be altered in a way that is undetectable to the human eye—a human still sees a stunning picture of a cat, but it causes the AI to recognize something completely different (`https://link.springer.com/article/10.1007/s11042-019-7262-8`).

However, a great deal of research is going in to advancing the science of deep learning. Some of the more notable advances include the following:

- **Learning with less data** (`http://doras.dcu.ie/22953/`) **or Few-Shot Learning** (`https://arxiv.org/abs/1903.02164`): Developing more efficient learning algorithms that can be trained with less data, or sometimes with as little as one training example (called **one-shot learning**)
- **Transfer learning** (`https://www.sciencedirect.com/science/article/pii/S0957417418305554`): Building a model for a new domain by transferring the model learned for another similar domain
- **Reinforcement learning** (`https://www.sciencedirect.com/science/article/pii/S1364661319300361`): Unsupervised learning using positive and negative reinforcement from the outcomes of a prior iteration in the learning cycle, but leveraging more judgmental forms of outcome interpretation
- **Federated distributed learning** (`https://arxiv.org/abs/1902.01046`): Building small models in a wide array of individual, typically resource-constrained, devices, and then federating all of those small models into one aggregate model
- **Recurrent neural networks** (`https://link.springer.com/chapter/10.1007/978-981-13-1966-2_49`) **and Neural Filters** (`https://arxiv.org/abs/1901.08096`): Incorporating long short-term memories and gated recurrent units to put more contextual attention on classification

Edge computing

By some estimates, there are approximately 15 billion intelligent devices on the market today. By intelligent devices, we mean anything that contains a computer and memory, typically connected to the internet, that can be used to do something interesting. Most often, these devices are out in the world where data is being produced (such as being expressed by humans, or captured from the human environment), and where actions are being taken. Virtually every modern TV, appliance, automobile, camera, (smartphone—but these are not counted in the 15 billion), factory and other industrial equipment, checkout terminal, ticket kiosk, **automated teller machine** (**ATM**), airplane, thermostat, and elevator, is built with an embedded computer. Even many brands of **light-emitting diode** (**LED**) lightbulbs have a small computer in them.

It is becoming increasingly important to deploy AI and other analytics onto these devices in order to do interesting things. For example, analytics on an assembly machine can be analyzed to predict its likelihood of failing in the next few days—giving factories a warning to schedule maintenance on that machine and saving hundreds of thousands of dollars in lost time if that machine were to fail in the middle of a production run. Cameras in your local ATM vestibule can detect whether someone is attempting to break into the ATM or rob a customer, so that the police can be contacted before the criminal can get away.

This is called **taking AI and analytics to the edge**.

However, these devices also pose some interesting challenges. Often, they are resource constrained, and so algorithms need to be optimized, and new model compression techniques need to be created to ensure that they don't exceed the available footprint of the device. Moreover, when you're dealing with billions, or even just thousands of devices, the task of determining which algorithm along with which model to place on which device, and then keeping those devices up to date when the models are retrained, can overwhelm administrators.

Automating the administrative process is essential and is another opportunity to apply AI.

Bias and ethics in AI

The major areas of concern that have surfaced include the potential for AIs to exhibit bias and the always-present danger that AI can be used to do harm.

Since AI relies on being trained, if the training data contains biases, then the resulting AI will learn that bias. A prominent example of this has surfaced with many of the visual recognition tools that are available now. Many of these tools have been trained with a very popular training set called **ImageNet**. This open source training set consists of over 14 million labeled pictures. But many of these pictures were taken in the Northern Hemisphere, and therefore the set is dominated with pictures of people of European descent (`https://internetofbusiness.com/mit-researchers-show-how-ai-systems-can-be-made-less-biased/`). Unfortunately, this means that many of these tools do a poor job of recognizing people from African and Indian countries.

More and more tools, algorithms, and techniques will surface over the next few years to help detect and combat bias in the datasets and also the algorithms that are deployed, which have been trained on those datasets. The Watson OpenScale offering that we discussed earlier in this chapter is one example of such a tool.

In the meantime, combating the potential for people to abuse this technology is gaining increasing attention. It will require a concerted effort among the technologists that create AI, those of us that consume the results of those technologies, and the regulatory authorities.

Compare the field of AI to the automobile—another incredibly useful tool. However, like many tools, cars can be abused and do much harm. But society has made significant strides in restricting the potential dangers of driving a car. For instance, auto manufacturers make annual improvements to increase the safety of their car—including, more recently, employing AI to help predict the potential for an accident, and maneuvering or even stopping the car to avoid collisions. Drivers are given extensive driving education and have established expectations and conventions for what is deemed to be acceptable driving behavior. Additionally, regulations have been introduced to introduce safer driving speeds and traffic control.

All of these devices will help establish the ethical use of AI in our society.

Robotics and embodiment

Since the very advent of AI, there has been a natural tendency to find an intersection between AI and robotics. Some of this probably is due to instinctual reasoning that, if AI is going to think like a human then perhaps it should be like a human. Other motivations are probably more basic, stemming from the fact that robots (even non-anthropomorphic, industrial robots) are inherently difficult to control—requiring various forms of complex logic to control their movements in a productive way. AI has become an obvious choice for supplying that logic.

But there may be an even deeper motivation that has been rarely touched on except for by the likes of Rodney Brooks (`https://people.csail.mit.edu/brooks/papers/AIM-1293.pdf`) and Cynthia Breazeal (`https://www.ted.com/talks/cynthia_breazeal_the_rise_of_personal_robots`).

As humans, we have evolved deeply-ingrained techniques for communicating with each other. Yes, we use our natural language—such as words to express our thoughts. But if you listen closely, you will begin to realize that we also use a wide range of vocal techniques to punctuate those words to draw attention to the more important syllables and terms—for instance, we use inflection, intonation, cadence, and timbre. These techniques are essential to convey clarity to our intended meaning. But then, we also use body language—such as eye contact, facial expressions, body movement, and hand and arm gestures—all to help resolve the ambiguity of our language or underpin the emotion of our expression.

When we're subjected to interacting with computers around the primary two-dimensions that have become our tradition— that is, a keyboard and display—we simply lose too much fidelity to our interaction; it doesn't feel natural. This very well may be why so many people are uncomfortable with using computers.

Robots—that is, social robots that exhibit a wider range of multidimensional interaction—have the potential to create a sense of presence in our lives. They are no longer just a piece of machinery in the corner of the room that is on when we turn it on, off when we turn it off, and otherwise neglected from our thoughts when we're not using it. A robot has the potential to exist in a more animated way, creating a stronger connection with our everyday needs.

We call this **embodiment**.

Quantum computing and AI

Jonathan Von Neumann began work on the blueprint for all modern computing in 1947 at the Center of Advanced Studies in Princeton, NJ—and similar work was also going on at approximately the same time at the University of Manchester, England, and other places, all based on the theories introduced by Alan Turing. Virtually every computer that we use is based on this architecture, which was introduced over 70 years ago. Even more exotic variations, such as GPUs, **field-programmable gate arrays** (**FPGAs**), and neuromorphic computers, are still based largely on the principles of digital binary encoding harnessing the physics of electromagnetism.

Quantum computing has emerged as the biggest breakthrough in computing architecture since the Von Neumann architecture. Quantum operates on the deeper principle of quantum mechanics, and more specifically, entanglement theory. We won't be able to get into the deeper aspects of how quantum computers work, but suffice to say that the major difference between Von Neumann and quantum computers is in its power and speed of computation. In its simplest form, Von Neumann computers operate in binary digits. Then, you string a set of bits together to represent a number or code. Each additional bit adds the power of 2 to the range of values represented by the string. When you string a set of **quantum bits (Qbits)** together, each bit adds the power of N to the range of values. Not only can you represent much larger values more efficiently, but the operations on those values are exponentially more powerful too—albeit, they are subject to the exotic nature of things that you can do in the quantum-mechanical world.

This, by itself, might suggest a strong benefit that quantum computers can bring to AI. After all, we know that AI algorithms are computationally complex. However, most of those algorithms are based on reasonably well-understood mathematics—and with heavy doses of matrix multiplication. Quantum computers, on the other hand, require a completely different set of logic to program them.

We will likely see a whole range of new algorithms developed as data scientists begin to grasp both the power and exotic nature of quantum computing (`https://www.sciencedirect.com/science/article/pii/S0004370209001398`).

The future of AI

When thinking about the future of AI, it is important to take stock of where we are. Throughout the course of this book, we have tried to make it clear that the vast majority of the capabilities in AI today are centered on recognition and classification tasks. That, in itself, is profound—representing the first thing any human does in any situation that requires reasoning.

However, just because you can recognize something and classify it doesn't mean that you truly understand its nature, its mechanics, its potential, or any number of other things that are important when reasoning about that thing. Likewise, recognition is a far cry from being able to reason deeply about a subject, or create new plans for tackling a problem, or imagining something that has never been created before. Additionally, none of these equates to the deeper motivations of emotion, such as guilt, happiness, frustration, anger, or love. All of these are aspects of human intelligence that we take for granted, but yet, when you get down to really thinking about it, is really very complicated.

There are many that have speculated about the future of AI—conjuring stories about the rise of AIs that exceed human intelligence and motivating all kinds of dystopian outcomes. Those stories are never more impactful than when put into a script for a movie.

In fact, this is an unrealistic future for AI. Yes, AI will continue to evolve and improve, and we will master the algorithms of deep reasoning with AI. However, it is unlikely that AI will evolve to mimic human intelligence. If AI evolves a higher intelligence, it won't be a form of intelligence that exceeds what humans already do exceptionally well; rather, it will be a different form of intelligence. We know this because we know something about the fundamental processes of evolution— both biological and technological. As humans, we have evolved our current form of intelligence from eons of environmental pressures—the techniques of reasoning, imagination, and creation that were necessary to survive the threats of the environment around us. In primeval human evolution, we developed the ability to sense danger and build weapons to protect ourselves. Then, we developed language as a means of communicating ideas and recipes to maximize our productivity and security. In modern times, we developed the means of organizing complex forms of governance to resolve conflicts and to enable cooperation at a large scale.

AI will never be subject to any of these pressures. Instead, AI will be subject to the pressures that technologists impose on it—through various experiments in adapting it to the problems prioritized by business, industry, and society. The evolutionary pressure on AI is to survive the need to be useful.

This brings us to a core tenet that these authors, IBM, and I think most of the industry has about AI. That is, it is not the objective of the AI industry to fully replicate the human mind, but rather to augment and amplify human cognition.

To think of this in other terms, consider this: if you examine the history of humankind and all of the tools that have had a lasting economic value on society, there is one thing that all of those tools have in common—they amplify human strength. The wheel, shovel, hammer, motor, hydraulics, and car—they all have had the effect of enabling people to do things that we couldn't do easily on our own. They've enabled us to build homes, harvest food, construct highways, and develop cities. They've given us the ability to connect people from all over the world and in every walk of life.

And that's the way to think about AI—it is a tool. It will enable us to process and refine the avalanche of information that is piling up around us at an ever-accelerating rate. It will help us to see patterns in data that will reveal new insights into curing diseases, eliminate hunger, make us more productive, leave a softer footprint on the earth, and even reach the stars. However, as a tool, it is in our hands to make the best use of it. It can eliminate many of the mundane tasks that we perform, and it can enable us to take on challenges that we simply couldn't without it, but only if we make good use of it.

Summary

Over the course of this book, we have exposed you to many of the services that Watson offers. We have shown you how to program the use of those services, and how to train them to adapt to your particular areas of interest. We have covered a lot of ground, but the fact is that we barely scratched the surface. In addition to the several services that we did not cover, there were also many other details about those services that we did cover. Hopefully, we gave you enough to get you started on your journey and with enough references to delve even further. We encourage you to explore on your own—to try new things, to look at what we left out, and to simply experiment.

In many ways, AI is a frontier like many others that have passed before it. It will undoubtedly unleash a wave of creativity and innovation. We should expect to see any number of improvements in our lives that will increase our productivity, help harness difficult tasks, and help solve problems that we simply couldn't before.

But AI is also different from anything before it as well. It is the closest to the one thing that is central to our very identity—our minds. It is the one technology that has demonstrated the ability to recognize things as we do. It can be taught new things simply by providing it an example. It continues to grow in value the more you use it—and those similarities can be frightening.

But, more than anything else, we have hopefully given you an insight into its true nature; to realize that AI is made up of algorithms taught by you and primarily about pattern recognition. AI is not a big, ethereal brain in the sky scooping up all of the world's knowledge and forming an increasingly powerful judgment of us with the logical conclusion that we are not worthy of our existence. Rather, AI is a tool that we can leverage to benefit ourselves, to bring strength to what we do, and to help us make better decisions than we could make ourselves without it.

Another Book You May Enjoy

If you enjoyed this book, you may be interested in these other books by Packt:

IBM Watson Projects
James D. Miller

ISBN: 9781789343717

- Build a smart dialog system with cognitive assistance solutions
- Design a text categorization model and perform sentiment analysis on social media datasets
- Develop a pattern recognition application and identify data irregularities smartly
- Analyze trip logs from a driving services company to determine profit
- Provide insights into an organization's supply chain data and processes
- Create personalized recommendations for retail chains and outlets
- Test forecasting effectiveness for better sales prediction strategies

Leave a review - let other readers know what you think

Please share your thoughts on this book with others by leaving a review on the site that you bought it from. If you purchased the book from Amazon, please leave us an honest review on this book's Amazon page. This is vital so that other potential readers can see and use your unbiased opinion to make purchasing decisions, we can understand what our customers think about our products, and our authors can see your feedback on the title that they have worked with Packt to create. It will only take a few minutes of your time, but is valuable to other potential customers, our authors, and Packt. Thank you!

Index

A

Anton-Babinski syndrome
  reference link 15
API key 71
application programming interface (API) 21
artificial intelligence (AI)
  about 20, 151, 223
  advances 229
  bias 232
  conversational systems 230
  deep learning (DL) 231
  edge computing 232
  embodiment 234
  ethics 232
  future 235
  Generative Adversarial Networks 229
  quantum computing 234
  robotics 233
artificial neural networks (ANNs) 11
automated teller machine (ATM) 232

B

Backpropagation through Time (BPTT) 137

C

Categories hierarchy
  reference link 159
classic NMT 137
classifier ID 71
Cloud Object Storage 142
cognitive computing 8
Compare and Comply (C&C) 224
computer
  about 82
  sound, playing through speaker 84
  using 152

context variables 46, 50
conventional computing
  limitations 8
  problem, solving 10
  transitioning, to cognitive computing 8
conversation application
  programming 52, 55, 57
conversational agent workspace
  creating 21
  sample application, building 24
conversational intents
  creating 25, 31
  entities, recognizing 33, 36, 38
custom model
  used, in NLU 200
Cynthia Breazeal
  reference link 234

D

DBpedia
  reference link 159
Deep Learning algorithms 65
dialog
  building 40, 42
  creating, for complex Intent using Frame Slots
  43
Discovery service 225

E

emotion detection
  reference link 161
empathy 113
English (en) 155
entities
  identifying, through annotators 38

F

field-programmable gate arrays (FPGAs) 235
Forkhead box Protein P2 (FOXP2) 9

G

Gated Recurrent Units (GRUs) 137
Graphical User Interface (GUI) 206
graphics processing units (GPUs) 227

I

IBM Cloud
  signing up 17
IBM Watson
  about 16
  hardware requisites 17
  software requisites 17
IBM
  features, emerging 60
image-recognition system
  creating 66
ImageNet 233
International Phonetic Alphabet (IPA)
  about 86
  reference link 86

J

JavaScript object notation (JSON) 58

K

knowledge catalog 227
Knowledge from Language Understanding and
  Extraction (KLUE) 170

L

Language Translation (LT) 128
languages
  translating, between Language Translator 138
light-emitting diode (LED) 232
Long Short-term Memory Neural Networks
  (LSTMs) 137

M

machine learning (ML)
  about 10, 63, 226
  Amazon 13
  classical computer vision 64
  cons 13
  deep learning, for computer vision 65
  Netflix 12
  supervised learning 12
  Tesla Autopilot 13
  unsupervised learning 12
  uses 12
  working 11
mathematical logic 8
Multilayer Perceptron Neural Network (MLPNN)
  132

N

Natural Language 128, 130
Natural Language Classifier (NLC)
  about 137, 142, 205, 218
  used, for categorizing text 140, 144, 149
Natural Language Translation 128, 131, 134, 136,
  138
Natural Language Understanding (NLU), concepts
  emotion 160
  entities 161
  keywords 164
  parts of speech 165
  relations 163
  semantic roles 164
  sentiment 161
Natural Language Understanding (NLU)
  about 151, 153, 216
  analyses, types 157
  annotate, preparing 168
  categories 158
  concepts 159
  custom model, used 200
  customizing 167
  documents, adding 174
  documents, as aside 175
  documents, loading into Watson Studio 177, 180
  documents, preparing in Watson Knowledge

Studio 176
literature, alternative sources 156
service 153
type system, creating 170, 174
NMT model
dictionary 140
training, with Watson 139
transfer learning 140

O

OpenScale
reference link 227

P

Personality Insights API
calling 123
poena 129
psycholinguistics 205
PyAudio package 214
Python
URL 52

Q

quantum bits (Qbits) 235
quantum computing
reference link 235

R

Rodney Brooks
reference link 234

S

sample application
building, from Watson Services 205
sentiment
complexities 114
SmarterEveryDay
reference link 9
software developer kit (SDK) 53
speech recognition service
acoustic model, customizing for Watson 108
batch process, leveraging 109
customizing 106
Watson's language model, customizing 106

speech service
telephone system 103
application 91
base models 104
computer, talking 92
speaker hesitations, dealing with 105
WebSockets interface, used for speech
recognition 96, 101
Speech Synthesizer Markup Language (SSML) 85
supervised learning 12
Symbolic Phonetic Representation (SPR) 86

T

Text analytics features
reference link 158
text
categorizing, Natural Language Classifier used
141, 144, 149
Tone Analyzer API
functionality 115
using 116, 119
transformation markups
reference link 86
TwitterService.py 217

U

unsupervised learning 12

V

voice
implementing 85
pronunciation, controlling 86
sounds-like customization, using 89
speech synthesis, customizing 87
streaming 89
timing 89

W

Watson Assistant
about 204
instance, creating 21
reference link 206
workspace, creating 21
Watson Language Translator

about 205
reference link 206
Watson Machine Learning (WML) 226
Watson Natural Language Understanding
about 205
reference link 206
Watson Personality Insights
about 205
reference link 206
Watson Personality
about 120
natural language, used to infer personality traits 121
Watson Services
about 204
application 206
application, setting up 219
concepts, summarizing 216
document, setting 214
entities, summarizing 216
entity personality, assessing 217
entity tone, assessing 217
entity, identifying 216
intent, determining 211
program flow 207
program, executing 218
recapping 204
sample application, building 205
text, classifying 218
text, translating 218
translate voice input 209
use-case 206
user, promoting for input 212
Watson Speech to Text
about 204

reference link 206
Watson Studio
about 226
annotations, performing 180, 183, 185, 187
coreferences 190
custom model, deploying to NLU 198, 200
documents, loading 177, 180
importance 189
reference link 226
training 193
Type System, editing 187
Watson Text to Speech
about 204
reference link 206
Watson Tone Analyzer 205
Watson Visual Recognition 204
Watson visual recognition
classifier, creating 66
classifier, testing 70
classifier, training 68
data, training 74
data, uploading 68
facial detection model, using 75, 79
instance, creating 66
Python application, creating to classify 71
Watson
Compare and Comply (C&C) 224
Discovery service 225
features 224
future 228
knowledge catalog 227
machine learning 226
OpenScale 227
services 224
Windows Subsystem for Linux (WSL) 17

www.ingramcontent.com/pod-product-compliance
Lightning Source LLC
Chambersburg PA
CBHW080635060326
40690CB00021B/4945